HELPING NETWORKS OF THE AGING AND RETIRED

Donald I. Warren

Studies in Health and Human Services
Volume 12

The Edwin Mellen Press
Lewiston/Queenston/Lampeter

Library of Congress Cataloging-in-Publication Data

Warren, Donald I.
    Helping networks of the aging and retired / Donald I. Warren.
       p. cm. -- (Studies in health and human services ; v. 12)
    Bibliography: p.
    ISBN 0-88946-137-6
    1. Aged--Social networks. 2. Retirees--Social networks.
I. Title. II. Series.
HQ1061.W34 1988
362.6--dc19

                              88-9014
                                  CIP

> This is volume 12 in the continuing series
> Studies in Health and Human Services
> Volume 12 ISBN 0-88946-137-6
> SHHS Series ISBN 0-88946-126-0

A CIP catalog record for this book is available
from The British Library.

The Edwin Mellen Press   The Edwin Mellen Press
P.O. Box 450   Box 67
Lewiston, NY 14092   Queenston, Ontario
USA   CANADA L0S 1L0

The Edwin Mellen Press, Ltd.
Lampeter, Dyfed, Wales
UNITED KINGDOM SA48 7DY

Printed in the United States of America

TABLE OF CONTENTS

They are aware of ceaseless deprivation and of everything being snatched from them...of being narrowed and lessened and ground out of their very personality. Tolstoy dealt with this terrible dismantling of the ego in his story "The Death of Ivan Ilyich," in which a man who has acquired everything necessary for his social indentification...has to watch himself stripped down until all that is left of him is a scream.

Ronald Blyth, *The View in Winter*

Our new lifestyle of being angry and outraged instead of resigned and docile is what empowers us. We have nothing to loose. Let's do something.

Maggie Kuhn, *The Gray Panther Manual*

ACKNOWLEDGEMENTS

This monograph was written as part of Service Contract #PLD0423279, under auspices of the Research Program, Center for the Study of the Mental Health of the Aging, Division of Special Mental Health Programs, National Institute of Mental Health.

INTRODUCTION

The present volume is directed at a better understanding of the often fragile patterns of help and social support available to the aging and retired in urban society. A total of nine cities and 59 neighborhoods were sampled in the overall project. Work was completed in 1976 following field interviews with 2,500 people in 1974. A follow-up re-interview involved 1,630 individuals.

While there is abundant evidence that the individual reaching age 65 or retirement sheds a number of the social contacts that characterize persons at other social stages in the life cycle, it is also important to recognize that many researchers have failed to point out that what does occur involves a multiple set of social linkages.

This volume is organized into twelve chapters with the initial one outlining in some detail the broad theoretical framework which has evolved from the original helping network study. In this discussion the concept of Problem Anchored Helping Networks (PAHNs) is introduced. Properties of this type of urban social tie are differentiated from such bonds as the primary group or intimate social networks. The rapid decline in problem-anchored networks with advanced age and retirement is seen as a major source of social isolation and a lowered quality of life for persons over 65 or those who are retired.

In Chapter II the basic analysis groups are described: a large number of persons who have been retired for at least one year; a small group of people who have recently retired; a similar group of persons who retired within one year of being initially interviewed; and a residential group of people who compose the remaining portion of the helping-network study sample.

Chapter III introduces a nature of problems including those of a crisis variety and a set of "recent concerns." These latter problems act as the central stimulus for evaluating helping network strength, form and effectiveness.

In Chapter IV the range of different kinds of helpers used in coping with problems is described--ranging from the spouse and kin helper to formal agencies.

Chapter V provides a detailed look at the variety of helping behaviors that each type of helper uses. These range from the more passive role of being a good listener to referral and direct action intervention.

Chapters VI and VII focus on the neighborhood. In the first instance attention is directed to neighbor social contacts and helping. In the second case it is the "social fabric"--both a typing of neighborhoods using a method developed in earlier studies and a set of perceptual indicators of what seniors and retirees think their neighborhood is like.

The importance of the wider community of residence is evaluated in Chapter VIII. Here the set of eight cities surrounding Detroit are compared using a measure of the "strength of helping networks." In addition, differences between the city--Detroit--and its suburbs is analyzed in terms of networks of seniors.

Chapter X addresses the important theoretical and practical issue of how different informal helpers--neighbors, kin, and friends--each play separate or overlapping roles in providing help for the aging and retired.

With Chapter XI a set of detailed propositions and hypotheses about helping and social integration are examined. This includes organizational and political participation by retirees and persons over age 65.

Chapter XII provides a review of the basic findings of the study and suggests some of the ways the research can illuminate issues of program effectiveness and planning in terms of outreach to the aging and the role of neighborhood-based interventions. A set of appendix tables and several operational steps in the field work are described at the back of the volume.

Finally, the reader should be cognizant of the original focus of the helping network study: to trace the use of informal and formal sources of aid for frequently encountered but not necessarily "crisis" problems. In this follow-up volume, focused on retirees and seniors, there are both similarities and differences in the findings as compared to the overall sample. Given the very limited size of the group focused upon here, statistical comparisons and conclusions reached from the data analyses we present must be viewed as exploratory rather than definitive.

> NOTE TO THE READER: A large amount of the tabular information presented in this volume involves percentage tables comparing four basic subgroups in the study. For values between 20 percent and 80 percent a difference of 10 percent is required to attain statistical significant at the .05 level. Percentages outside of 20 and 80 require a 6 percent difference for significance.

CHAPTER I

A THEORY OF THE HELP-SEEKING PROCESS

For many decades we, as a society, failed to understand the ecosystem of our surrounding physical environment. Similarly, we have only recently begun to investigate and identify the components that make up the social fabric of human communities. This fabric is woven from the complex interdependencies that are the formal and informal helping systems of our society.

Increasingly, our highly trained and dedicated professional helping institutions have begun to recognize that they alone cannot provide the resources and social supports which are so vital to the well-being of the communities in which we live. There is an invisible partnership of which they are unaware: it is a web woven by a combination of neighbors, friends, co-workers, relatives, voluntary agencies and formal human service organizations.

Collins (1973:46) described "natural neighbors," who comprise a natural system of service delivery, as a "...network of relationships in which individuals seeking a specific service find it, without professional intervention." A number of studies were reviewed by Collins and Pancoast (1974) which indicated that the frequency of contact with friends, relatives, and neighbors is an important factor in providing support and help within natural networks. Collins and Pancoast stress that:

Informal, spontaneous helping activities occur so often all around us that they usually pass without notice. Except for spectacular rescues, instances of helping behavior are much less likely to be reported than are instances when bystanders failed to act on behalf of someone in distress (1974:24).

In an effort to identify indigenous helping activities among various age groups, Patterson (1971, 1974, 1977) studied a population in a rural Kansas county ranging in age from sixteen to eighty-three. Her major research findings indicated that the type of helper (natural helper versus professional) was an important factor in the helping process in terms of: 1) type of problem encountered; 2) type of helping approaches or techniques utilized; and 3) the type of relationship between the helper and the helped (1977:164). An important difference between natural helpers and professional helpers is that the natural helpers provided both support and helping "because they cared rather than out of expectations of future rewards" (1977:165).

Networks operate by: a) giving emotional support, b) providing specific information, c) filling in where a close relationship is severed by death, illness, divorce or separation, etc., d) helping identify arenas of good professional help, and e) serving in place of professionals when they are not trusted or not available.

Basic to our theory is that bypassing existing helping structures within the community may systematically lower the adaptive capacity of many human populations and weaken those indigenous resources which in times of crisis may be the only ones available and operative.

Helping network analysis is not simply looking at the direct contact that an individual makes with a helper. An individual is part of a system of networks that can provide resources or pathways of help. The individual may not know directly about useful help, but he or she may be in a context in which other people know about a resource and can provide that information. It is an issue of community social integration – patterns in which people relate to each other and to the community as a whole, and ways in which resources are coordinated and used for the common good – and this can be contrasted with the disintegration of resources and links.

Seeking and receiving help from others in American society is constrained by dominant cultural values emphasizing a propensity for self-reliance and avoidance of dependency upon others except among the very young and very old in society. The necessity of having to seek help may, therefore, result in risk to one's ability to perform essential tasks or may entail having to admit failure in some aspect of one's life. These situations have been related to a number of psychological and social consequences resulting from help-seeking behaviors.

In the work of Robert Weiss (1974) the "provision of social relations" becomes a major focus of the social support and helping process. The severing of a social tie or the failure to establish a "helping network" may be seen as a major source of risk to mental health as well as to general well-being. In light of the basic assumption about the role of helping, the absence of helpers might be considered a barrier that the individual has in coping with a range of problems in daily life.

A major function of informal social networks is to provide social support which acts to integrate people sociably into meaningful primary group relationships as well as the provision of helping behaviors when group members experience problems. Weiss (1974:20) points out that failure to establish such relationships may result in "social and emotional isolation." He defines social integration as the network of relationships in which participants share common concerns. Once one is socially integrated into such a network, it functions as follows:

> Membership in a network of common concern relationships permits the development of pooled information and ideas and a shared interpretation of experiences. It provides, in addition, a *source of companionship and opportunities for exchange of service*, especially in the area of common interests. The network offers a base for social events and happenings, for social engagement and social activity. In the absence of such relationships life becomes dull, perhaps painfully so [1974:23 – emphasis added].

While these researchers emphasize the psycho-social barriers to seeking and receiving help for problems, others attribute differential patterns of help-seeking to various cultural and sociodemographic factors. Addressing both the psychological and social aspects of help-seeking, Gurin (1960:xx) and his colleagues noted salient features in groups that sought help:

This group that "went for help" was dominated by women, younger persons, and the better educated. These types, as we have observed, are inclined to be introspective, self-critical, and more concerned about themselves.

To summarize, it appears that seeking help for problems involves a multiplexity of psychological and sociocultural factors which can be construed as barriers to effective helping resources for various segments of the population. Thus, many people with problems never reach professional helping resources and never receive help. At best, these people must look for assistance within the context of informal social support networks. The critical question is, to whom do these people turn to for help and what kind of "help" is both available and provided?

Social Support Versus Helping

Studies concerned with the nature and utilization of social networks tend to agree that networks operate by providing socio-emotional support for their members, filling in where a close relationship is severed by death, illness, divorce, or other life crises, helping to identify or recommend where to get professional help, and serving in place of professionals when they are not available or not trusted. The mere existence of social networks may function to banish the isolation which can itself be a source of other personal and social problems.

It is clear from the social network literature that "social support networks" can serve a variety of individual psychological functions for maintaining "social integration" within the network and helping mechanisms for coping with problems. What is less clear is the conceptual and operational definition of these social support networks. An immediate question that arises is what is the difference between "social support" and "helping"? We suggest that social support is not necessarily the same as helping behavior and, further, social support is not synonymous with social interaction and network contacts. Yet the concepts of social support and helping have been used interchangeably and the differences that may exist between them have been largely neglected in the literature.

High rates of social interaction do not guarantee that help will be available from other people. Assessing the relationship between "perceived" support for "everyday" versus "emergency" problems, Wellman and his colleagues (1971:27) found an association between frequency of contact and support for "everyday" problems, but a much weaker association for "emergency" help:

> Our data shows a strong positive association between frequency of contact and the provision of support. The association is somewhat weaker in the case of emergency support, revealing the existence of a number of intimates who are contacted relatively infrequently but who can be called upon for help in times of need (1971:27).

The Problem-Tracking Approach

Various methods for tackling problems in terms of analyzing the processes by which people seek help have been referred to as "client careers" (Goffman, 1961). These processes represent different behavior patterns anchored in some combination of preference for help sources. The notion of "career" has also been defined as a series of stages or phases a person passes through toward some end point or goal which involves defining problems, sorting them out, and seeking help for problems at various stages of problem development. Moreover, this definition of "career" implies a series of events and corresponding help-seeking behavior patterns shared by several people concurrently. As Roth (1963:93) points out, "...When many people go through the same series of events, we speak of this as a career and the sequence and timing of events as their current time tables."

Tracking problems based on the availability and nature of people's support and referral networks provides personal road maps we call "pathways of help-seeking."[2] This approach suggests that, after initial self-perception and definition (diagnosis) of a problem, people will often consult with significant others or "informal" people for concurrence or referral. Essentially, the careers or pathways of help-seeking involve a preference for help sources, availability of various kinds of professional or nonprofessional resources, the nature of the person's informal support and referral networks, and various personal and social characteristics of the individual.

The specific help-seeking behavior people will adopt is dependent, we suggest, upon a number of psychological and sociocultural factors. These factors may be categorized into four major groups and discussed in terms of their influence on illness or help-seeking behavior. They are: 1) the social status of the individual including such demographic characteristics as age, sex, marital status, socioeconomic status, type of disability, and sociocultural setting; 2) the individual's view of health including self-conception, cultural values regarding health, views toward medical practice and practitioners, inclination to adopt the sick role, and information about medical problems; 3) the existence, nature, and utilization of informal support and referral networks; and 4) the nature and types of life crises, corresponding stress associated with these crises, and the means by which the individual adapts to or copes with these life stresses.

The way an individual seeks out help to handle problems or crises is dependent in part upon how the problem is subjectively perceived. Apart from any pathological condition, the course that the individual will follow is influenced by the social behavior brought on by a specific problem. This has even been referred to as "illness behavior": "the way in which symptoms are perceived, evaluated, and acted upon by a person who recognizes some pain, discomfort, or other signs of organic malfunction" (Mechanic and Volkert, 1961:52). Thus, how one "acts" upon these perceptions and evaluations determines to a large extent the specific career or pathway one will choose to handle the problem.

Help-Seeking: A Network Process

What leads one person to choose a particular agency, professional, or helping resource and another person to reject these and make completely different choices? This questions is a difficult one to answer and yet has not been looked at extensively or very systematically by agencies or social researchers.

From that vague, indeterminant point at which a problem begins, to the receipt of effective help is often a long road. The symptomatic manifestation of psychological or social problems represents the culmination of a long period of accumulated symptoms, events, or behaviors and not the initial onset of a problem. Differences in patterns will be due to some combination of variables, including preferences for help sources, availability of various kinds of professional and non-professional help, personal and local values, the character of a person's informal support and referral network, and various other personal and social characteristics of the individual. Particular populations will, in turn, be characterized by the predominance of certain routing or decision pathways.

It is useful to consider four levels of help sources of service delivery systems that individuals may utilize. These include:

The Lay (Informal) Service System – This phenomena includes the friendship and kinship network in which an individual is involved and which can be mobilized for help in problem definition, referral, and direct service. It also embodies selected community members who have developed a reputation for help-giving.

Quasi-Formal and Self-Help Systems – This includes voluntary organizations, help-giving activities of churches and community groups whose primary function is not to operate as a service agency, and various local community services which do not have the credentials or wide community acceptance of formal service agencies. Such operations often service a limited local community and, although they may employ or be connected with one or two professionals, the bulk of their work is carried on by non-professional staff.

Professional Service Agencies – These organizations operate primarily as social services. They have credentials and are generally recognized. Their staffs are for the most part professional and they service a wide community.

Inter-Organizational Relationships – The combination and coordination of two or more agencies, either formal or quasi-institutional, creates a special set of activities, structures, and administrative problems which shapes the design and implementation of service delivery. In some cases, these coordinated activities are established as separate administrative units and essentially form an agency of agencies. In other cases, the coordination is short term to meet immediate problems and the relationship is dissolved when the issue which led to its establishment is resolved.

To date, we find in the literature many studies dealing retrospectively with help-seeking behavior. That is, after someone has sought help, networks are plotted by which these same individuals chose a course of action resulting in differential patterns of help-seeking.

Critical to the research strategy of our own study is the argument that help-seeking is importantly altered and shaped by the social milieu as well as an individual's social background and personality. In addition, it is asserted that such differences in helping networks that are available or utilized, in turn, affect the capacity of the individual to "handle" problems with greater or lesser amounts of outside help.

A Conceptual Typology of Individual Problems

In their "balance theory" of the roles of primary groups and bureaucratic organization, Eugene Litwak and Henry Meyer distinguish between two kinds of tasks, "uniform" and "non-uniform."[3] Non-uniform tasks are those events which are unique or idiosyncratic and non-recurring. These kinds of problems may require expert knowledge. By their nature (according to Litwak and Meyer's theory) these kinds of problems are most suited to be dealt with by primary groups. Uniform tasks, on the other hand, are most suited to solution by bureaucracies. These tasks usually involve recurring events that can be broken into components, are solvable by specific rules, and, most critically, require expert knowledge and a complex division of labor.

Building upon the notions of Litwak and Meyer, Warren and Clifford (1974) developed the concept of "invoked expertise." The term "invoked expertise" refers to the level of technology or specialized knowledge seen necessary and then invoked by a person to cope with a problem. Using the three core elements of this concept, problems can be dimensionalized and distinguished along a continuum of "high," "medium," and "low." The three core elements are: 1) complexity of the elements of the problems and the life space involved; 2) extensivity of knowledge of technology relevant to the problem solution; and 3) normative association with the problem.

For example, a low-expertise problem is characterized by the fact that: 1) it requires the observation and control of many (possibly complex) ancillary conditions, relationships, and behaviors for which an expert cannot practically be utilized; 2) expert knowledge, even when highly developed, is present for only a part of the problem or a particular phase, i.e., expert knowledge is lacking in the core content of the evaluation of the problem's emergence, definition, or resolution; and 3) there is limited or no agreement among experts or subgroups in the general population on the applicability of particular expertise to the problem and on the definition of the problem (particularly normative). Low-invoked expertise problems involve the presence of all these elements; high-invoked expertise problems, the absence or reverse of these propositions; medium-invoked expertise problems will involve a varying mix of presence and absence of the criteria. Table I-1 elaborates on these three categories and gives some typical examples.

From the above discussion and Table I-1 several particularly important points should be noted. At the high-expertise level there is wide agreement on the definition and labeling of something as a "problem." By the same token, there is a low normative and emotional loading on most issues surrounding the problem. At the low expertise end of the continuum there is not only disagreement on definition, but even disagreement as to when a problem exists. Also, these types of problems are generally accompanied by strong normative and emotional involvements. Often there exist jurisdictional disputes among professions over who has proprietary "rights" to a problem area. There may be competing claims of success and efficacy by both professional helpers and non-professional helpers and organizations. These situations become more manifest as one moves from "high" to "low" on the scale. In high-expertise problems these conflicts are lowest. In low-expertise problems there may be low manifest conflict but

10

TABLE I-1
A TYPOLOGY OF SOCIAL PROBLEMS BASED ON THE LEVEL OF INVOKED EXPERTISE

High Expertise (Low Community Variance)	Medium Expertise (Medium Community Variance)	Low Expertise (High Community Variance)
Problem has a well-defined sophisticated technology associated with its detection and resolution, although debate may occur regarding its most efficient solution "design" or engineering.	Problem has an actively developing technology, but with widely varying success levels in application, or competing approaches have similar limited effectiveness. Differing definitions, analytical frameworks, and discipline and specialization origins; various operational "models" are rampant. Little is known about long-term effects of solutions.	Problem either lacks formal recognition in professional taxonomies or is included with other problems. It tends toward diffuse or non-specific etiology or symptom syndrome. In particular, it lacks a treatment modality or technology that has been well tested, let alone refined.
Problems of social values are minimal: high consensus is present both from experts and non-experts as to the need for action. Debate centers on the timing, equity, and speed of implementing a solution.	Problems are often in a state of flux and redefinition. The experts can't agree, and formal agencies vie over proper jurisdictional lines. Rival labels are used to describe the seriousness of the issue, although there is widespread recognition that "something" should be done in the short run.	Both initial and ongoing effects are closely tied to traditional social values or norms which are created and sustained by significant primary groups.
Problem is often identified with a highly specialized field within a profession, and may be treated entirely within the confines of a formal agency.	Non-expert elements may be significant in symptom remediation and treatment.	Specialized expertise is only ancillary to problem definition and coping. Perception and response are highly idiosyncratic, and not readily visible to formal social institution. Regulation of behavior depends heavily on shared local values and "moral suasion."
Actions and efforts by non-experts or advocate groups cannot greatly change the nature of the problem or provide a solution that is at variance with the known data.		Regardless of the perceived severity of the problem or consensus as to longer run effects as seen by specialists, major social values and the nonuniform character of the problem as experienced by individuals makes concerted formal action of limited value.

Table I-1 (cont)

Selected Examples of Health and Family Issues

1.	Hypertensive heart disease	1.	Alcoholism	1.	Life cycle role transition (women entering work force after absence, men retiring)
2.	Sickle cell anemia	2.	Simple depressive psychosis		
3.	Schizophrenia	3.	Job related emotional stress	2.	Youth-parent tensions
4.	Organically based child	4.	Control of smoking	3.	Leisure malaise (due to shortened work week, etc.)
5.	Prenatal child/mother care	5.	Obesity		
6.	Cancer detection and treatment	6.	Post-operative and general physical therapy	4.	Common cold effects
7.	Stroke	7.	Career selection	5.	Consumer purches by families (house, furnishings, car, appliances)
		8.	Marital discord		
		9.	Family planning	6.	Family budgeting
				7.	Post-natal family adjustment

Source: Donald Warren and David Clifford, "Invoked Expertise and Neighborhood Type: Two Critical Dimensions in the Coordination of Bureaucratic Service Organizations and Primary Groups." Paper read at the annual meeting of the American Sociological Association, 1974.

much latent or incipient conflict. In the case of medium-expertise problems, conflicts among professionals, among non-professionals, and various specialist areas are likely to be most apparent.

Further, in differentiating problems one can note the fact that specialized bureaucratic or service structures exist to treat particular types of problems using particular methods. Specialization, standardization, and social control of this sort is likely to be greatest with problems described as "high invoked expertise." Those problems which fall into the middle, "medium invoked expertise," on the other hand: 1) often lie within a disputed frontier of professional expertise and, thus, are viewed as the "property" of several specialities; and 2) are reflective of ambiguous or limited success when viewed in comparison to "high-expertise" problems. In the case of low-expertise problems, the very emergence of an issue as a "problem" may be problematic when viewed from the standpoint of either the professionals on the one hand, or the lay community on the other. Thus, the problem-labeling process could be viewed at this level in its most diverse and fundamental form.

Central to the "problem level invoked" concept is the proposition that expertise and jurisdiction over a problem area (or task area within the treatment of a particular problem) can be highly dynamic. Problems can move both up and down the scale. One need only observe the medical profession where, historically, the trend was for doctors to assume ever increasing areas of responsibility for medical care, and then, with either the routinization of some tasks or the development of competing technologies, the diffusion of some tasks to other new professions and para-professions. An example of the conflict surrounding some medium-expertise problems is alcoholism, where both professionals and non-professionals using a variety of "techniques" claim efficacy.

With this typology in hand a selection of "problems" can be made which will provide comparable stimuli for the study of coping responses of different individuals and groups. The problems from the same level of expertise will be those most legitimate for comparison of coping.

The Choice of Problems for Analysis of Helping Patterns

There are three reasons for differentiating among types of problems: 1) the role of primary group or informal helping systems in coping may vary considerably by problem type; 2) some communities or population groups may be more able to provide significant coping resources than others, depending on the type of problem; and 3) the involvement of professional helpers will vary systematically across problem type regardless of community or demographic differences. Thus, if one wants to focus on informal, non-professional helping (involving the widest variance due to community character) one needs to examine those problems which allow and even require the greatest involvement by informal helpers and non-professional community resources.

"Medium-" and, in particular, "low-" invoked expertise problems may be handled entirely outside the formal helping and service delivery systems of the community. Also, they cannot, by definition, be effectively dealt with solely by formal professional organizations. Additionally, even where such problems have a high degree of visible and legitimate professional expertise associated with their initial labeling or identification, their treatment, remission, and maintenance are often largely functions of the informal helping systems embodied in local neighborhoods, networks of neighbors, friends, co-workers, and other community institutions.

Those problems labeled medium to low expertise offer the richest ground for examining variance in informal, non-professional systems of helping – and therefore of the "natural helping networks" of individuals. We now turn to the focal research design and its subsequent finding where "level of invoked" expertise serves as a sensitizing concept to the understanding of how helping networks function.

Problem-Anchored Helping Networks

The research conducted in the Detroit metropolitan area has provided – beyond its original intent – a basis for defining a distinct "network" in which the linkage between friends, neighbors, relatives, co-workers and professional agency helpers is defined by the reported "talking about a recent concern or problem." Specifically we have these distinguished as Problem-Anchored Helping Networks (PAHNs):

> Social contacts that an individual makes with any number of other persons (not necessarily intimates or status equals) with the results that a particular "problem" or "concern" or "crisis" is discussed and advice or help provided.

Problem-anchored helping networks (PAHNs) are heterogeneous in composition and can readily expand in a chain-like fashion outward to other networks. The individual thus typically belongs to several networks simultaneously. These networks are linked only in terms of the common link of that one ego and are not cohesive in any other way. In terms of an institutional or structural notion, these networks are "always there" even if a given individual does not utilize them. To this degree, problem-anchored helping networks are the set of helpers sought out by a given individual whether these are situated in a working unit of an organization, a neighborhood setting or a voluntary organization. These are social ties which depend on a population interacting on the basis of a common behavioral setting and a specific problem. Mutual aid is given and/or received with regard to problems confronted in one's daily life.

The Function of PAHNs Within Ongoing Social Support Systems

Up to now, we have treated PAHNs as if they were a separate social structural entity. Yet they may also be seen from a different perspective as well: namely that PAHNs are a social process that occurs within and between existing ties. In this view, specifically, helping networks (PAHNs) are an intrinsic component of any given informal social bond. Often they serve as the boundary-defining and external contact points of such structures.

Social contact implies the potential for helping behaviors defined by the existence of a matrix of informal social contacts. These informal networks provide a social milieu in which proximity and social interaction suggest a probability that social support and helping activities may be available from these relationships.

Social support and problem-specific helping should be viewed as separate social-network functions. They provide distinct activities to individuals who experience recent concerns or crises. Thus, social-support activities are concerned with social-emotional feedback, reinforcement, providing for the release of negative affects, and enhancing social integration. Problem-specific helping activities, on the other hand, are based on specific actions taken on the part of informal "helpers" to provide individuals with problem-coping mechanisms.

A typology of functional relationships within the small group context was posited by Parsons and Bales (1955) and illustrates the "balance" between interpersonal ties. The "task specialist" is concerned primarily with "instrumental" operations within the group – how to reach a specific goal – while the "socioemotional specialist" concentrates on the "expressive" interactions keeping the group together and undertaking motivation to participate (1955:151). Thus, within any group (or network), there are those who provide predominantly instrumental resources oriented toward achieving the goals or purposes of the group and those who offer primarily expressive support.

We submit that within any given social network there will be a balance between expressive and instrumental activities provided by all of the members in the network. The important issue is that the "nature of the interpersonal" ties will determine to a large extent the predominance of "expressive" versus "instrumental" network activities. We would expect that social networks characterized as loose-knit are more likely to feature a predominance of instrumental activities oriented toward problem-solving tasks. Close-knit social networks, on the other hand, are more likely to provide expressive support to members of the social network oriented toward sociability, network integration, and coping efforts. In order to achieve effective problem-solving capabilities, however, both expressive and instrumental skills must be present in the social network. The helping behaviors of "referring" and "taking action" are good examples of "instrumental helping" versus the more expressive "listening" or "asking questions."

While the various functions of informal social networks are viewed as separate activities, they are interdependent. Thus, it is unlikely that problem-specific (instrumental) helping will occur within informal social networks where some degree of social interaction and expressive support does not already exist. An exception might be in an emergency situation. Moreover, it is impossible for either social support or helping activities to occur if individuals do not come into contact with one another initially and share at least some degree of social interaction.

Closeness versus Helping

Helping Networks (PAHNs) are an intrinsic potential within any given informal tie–primary group, social network, etc. The idea of "intimate" social networks connotes a rather different social bond. As such, PAHNs are a *process*-focused social tie more than an enduring structure of normatively defined social links. Thus, primary groups have intrinsic functions that are "expressive" as well as "instrumental." Such "close-knit" ties may be more readily considered social systems in which a balance of task and expressive interaction occurs. PAHNs are initially at least based only on instrumental behaviors which are their raison d'être. They are intermittent, ephemeral and lack shared identity.

Self-conscious helping may be antithetical to the sociability, expressive support, and reinforcement provided by close friendship. That is, intimate social ties which become dominated by excessive requests for problem-specific helping behaviors which introduce individuals to other informal social contacts (i.e., through referral) may lead to the establishment of new or expanded intimate networks. Yet in a given "intimate network" help and sociability are separate from and often in an adversarial relationship.

As the "instrumental" helping process increases, the "expressive" aspects of a social network or primary group may be weakened. Thus, a duality is present which may often be maintained in coexistence by a rough "balancing."

The persistence or duration of a PAHN is a function of the type of instrumental help provided. If it is able to generate referral, new knowledge or "treatment" of a problem then it is likely to be used again–either for the same or a new problem. Any friendship dominated by helping tends to corrode, overspecialize, and render the relationship exploitive.

Basic to our argument is the assumption that people turn to intimates for help because they are socially proximal and not because of their helping expertise.

Social Cohesion and Helping Patterns

The term "social integration" refers to the ties between parts of a group – what holds it together in the face of pressures and challenges, both external and internal. Applied at the community level, sociologists from Durkheim to Parsons have seen the chief mechanisms for integration as political parties, interested groups and, particularly, the juridical system. But this usage of the term is applied at a highly formal level of analysis. Community integration can be examined at a more informal level. The concept as commonly applied refers to stresses related to serious social, societal and personal problems and "extreme" circumstances.

The "low-invoked" (grass roots) expertise problems used to elicit the coping and helping experiences of retired and aging people in the Detroit area study represent the day-to-day ups and downs and stresses with which people must cope. The helping relationships in which people are imbedded are the "glue" that helps hold them and society together. These patterns of "social integration," as one author states, "refer to the ways in which individuals relate to one another and to the community as well as to the ways in which resources are coordinated for the common good" (Klein, 1968:106).

PAHNs are One Expression of "Organic" Solidarity

In contrast to other informal social ties, PAHNs do not require that a named intimate provide the basis of "networking." Thus, in fact, the Detroit research deals with links between social arenas such as neighborhood, workplace, and formal agencies and not specific persons located in these settings. From one time to another the problem-experiencing individual may use a different neighbor or the same one – the key point is that the social arena of the neighborhood is utilized.

In Chart I-1 we have depicted the "indirect" networking which is the PAHN social process. For any given "behavior arena," one can visualize a

PATTERNS OF INFORMAL HELPING
NETWORKS

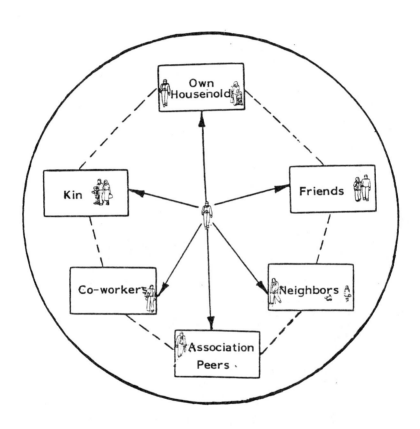

"pool" of potential helpers whose capacity to form a network is based on the single individual who seeks aid in that setting. To the degree that the same person also goes to other arenas for problem coping, these otherwise disparate spheres are tied together. This process is one of very indirect versus direct social integration. Neither the seeker of help not the giver of aid need be in a close social relationship for linkage to occur. Specifically we have argued that:

> Community and individual health or well-being (or effectiveness in problem coping) is a function of the range of informal social ties utilized by members and the diversity of pattern characterizing a population;

> a pivotal role in the linkage between varieties of informal social ties is played by problem-anchored helping networks: they tie in with both loose, and tight, knit patterns of a given population group or individual; and

> the major dynamic of change or shift in the balance of loose, or tight, knit ties is to be located in the role of problem-anchored helping networks.

All of the brokerage roles we have ascribed to problem-anchored helping networks may be viewed as sources of strength in regard to individual well-being. Thus, it may be argued that it is not simply the variety of loose- and tight-knit ties alone (that is, the volume and diversity of social ties which makes for a healthy community) but the fact that they can be interlinked through the pivotal role of one type of social tie – the problem-anchored helping network. Without this knitting or bridging form of social network, the depersonalizing and transient character of loose-knit ties might indeed produce the negative effects on individual well-being and community strength that have been ascribed to them.

The essential point is this: loose-knit ties in the context of the availability of problem-anchored helping networks have a potential for being qualitatively more significant than if loose ties are treated in isolation. Moreover, helping networks alone are not the basis of community. Instead, PAHNs are the bridging mechanism that ties primary groups and social networks all considered as Informal Social Ties to formal organizations and generally to all secondary groups in society. This process is depicted by the diagram of Chart I-2.

CHART I-2
DIFFERENTIAL NATURE OF SICN AND PAHN
VARIATIONS OF INFORMAL SOCIAL TIES

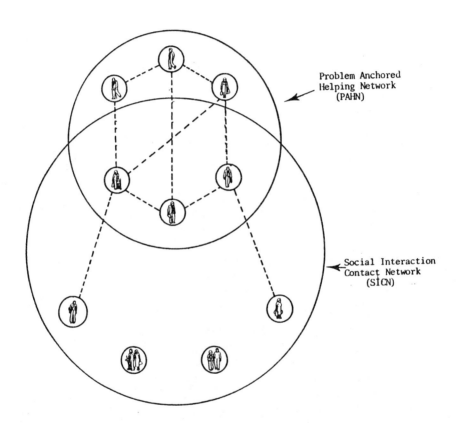

If PAHNs are viewed as emergent in the normal communication within all forms of informal social bonds, the critical interaction is not between conscious, instrumental help-seeking but the potential for help to be realized out of the dynamics of social interaction *per se*. Thus, one may ask: To what extent does the existence of a social network provide a capacity for a person to meet new problems or challenges? To what degree is the "sense of belonging" to a social network psychologically satisfying in the same way that knowing that one belongs to an identified, recognized, geographically demarcated or social observable ethnic, class or occupational community? To what degree is the sociability of social networks a substitute for participation in the "larger community"–the nation-state, the "greater culture," etc.?

Some of the network studies suggest that the traditional "cosmopolitan" is the same as the social networker–informed, powerful by virtue of "connections" and able to flexibly adapt and to anticipate the next change or problem to be confronted; traditional solidarities of close -knit neighborhoods or closed primary groups cannot. Yet "social networks" often describe very parochial, insular kinds of patterns which may be helpful to the individual, but that may be isolating from a broader community. There is a danger that, to the extent a person relies exclusively on the intimate social network, that individual is less likely to take an active coping stance toward a number of broad social problems. If one is totally immersed in social networks, one may not have energy to participate in the wider community.

The helping-network study suggests that mere "social support" is not what the individual wants when they face daily problems, or even life crises. Instead, often what is sought is a different way of looking at the world, some specific resources–"while I'm thinking about going back to school it's nice that you are telling me that it is a good idea, but can you show me how I can actually apply?" And if I have some kids to take care of, "what kind of schedule can I work out?" "Is there a day care service somewhere around that I can use in connection with that?" "As a good friend you tell me I ought to back to school; but how am I going to do it?"

Being part of a helping network can direct an individual's attention to the needs of others in a community. Yet the helping that is indigenous to a community is not self-conscious or necessarily instrumental – it grows out of sociability; it becomes an expression of a potential, unspoken reciprocity. That we all may become referral agents in problem helping is one indicator of community health. From one perspective a "problem-anchored helping network" is based on entering into the large community through a series of steps or pathways (combinations of resources) that are not based on an intimacy, but simply on the sharing of the same problem with another individual.

A Summary Perspective

We began this chapter with a specific idea in mind: that the helping process of an individual must be placed in a larger context – that of the social cohesion of the contemporary urban community. After exploring the ideas of theorists who have attempted to define what is the basis of that solidarity, we presented a series of propositions about the specialized functions and interrelations of several different varieties of informal social bonds and the pivotal role of helping networks. We then went on to depict the process of problem coping as a built-in function of community life. We further specified the nature of problem-anchored "helping networks" (PAHNs) as a separable basis of "organic" linkages within a given population or geographic locale. In addition, several propositions – more accurately, hypotheses – were generated to identify the meaning of helping "symbiotic" ties between individuals.

Our original point of departure – unlike elements coexisting – now emerges in more specific form. In fact, it has three facets: a "balance" of helping systems from informal to formal; a "balance" of helping content – "social support" and instrumental aid; and problem-anchored helping as a bridge between close-knit social groups and very free-floating, occasional social contacts. Each of these and all of them expressed the variety of "organic" diversification found in urban life. They are expressions of "social cohesion" but in often very indirect ways.

In the present analysis we shall apply the conceptual schema outlined in this chapter to the life situation of seniors and retirees who formed a part of the larger "helping-network" sample. The findings represent a tentative testing of key hypotheses and provisional validation of the utility of the ideas that have been exposited. It is to this task that the content of subsequent chapters is devoted.

CHAPTER II

CHARACTERISTICS OF THE RETIREES AND SENIORS IN THE HELPING-NETWORK SURVEY

Study Design and Sampling

The helping-network study had three major research goals. The first of these was to describe the importance of the local community and neighborhood in terms of providing help and problem-solving resources. At the same time, the focus of locality implied that such attachments were themselves a source of well-being for the individual. The second goal of the study was to obtain a more complete picture of the types of choices people make when they experience a problem and are seeking help. Such an inquiry also requires that we pursue what kinds of things are in fact, sought in any "helping transaction." Examples include emotional support, specific information or a new way of thinking about a persistent problem. A methodology for measuring such variability in what constitutes help was developed. Thirdly, the study was aimed at an implicit evaluation of the degree to which people used and trusted various types of helping resources – formal agencies as well as the next-door neighbor.

To carry out the substantive task of the study several different data-gathering techniques were employed. A central source of information was the systematic survey interviews that were conducted. An initial "baseline" sample included over 2,500 persons. They were chosen in two ways. First a one percent random sample of eight communities surrounding Detroit was undertaken. At the same time, a completely separate representative sample of 32 non-Detroit and 27 Detroit neighborhoods was drawn. This was based on a "walking distance" definition of neighborhood using the local elementary school district as a sampling unit. Approximately 40 adults, heads of household or their spouse were interviewed in this way.

All of the information obtained in the helping-network study was gathered during 1974 and 1975. A staff of professional interviewers as well as a number of trained neighborhood observers provided the personnel to complete the research.

A number of the neighborhoods had been included in an earlier 1969 study comparing Black and White areas. In both the municipal community sample of 770 persons and the neighborhood samples the vast majority of persons were moderate income rather than affluent. The Detroit SMSA was typified in this way. The 59 neighborhoods yielded approximately 1,700 completed interviews with adults in these areas. Each interview lasted an average of 80 minutes.

The baseline survey instrument focused on six basic areas. 1) A series of individual concerns related to job, personal attitudes, crime, and change in family and life-cycle roles such as retirement, additional schooling, etc. Where a person had experienced a problem recently, we charted the pathway by which they sought help. We asked them not only what people (ranging from primary-group members to professionals) they talked to, but also what happened in the interaction with the "helper." 2) Use of professional helping agencies. 3) Occurrence in the past year of critical life-events such as major illness, death of a family member, loss of job, etc. 4) A checklist of psychosomatic symptoms and other questions on health. 5) Helping roles played by different family members. 6) Neighborhood social interaction, perceived resources and use of actual resources.

One of the unique parts of the helping-network study was the utilization of a follow-up survey paralleling the original 1974 interview. A total of 1,531 persons were successfully contacted one year later. This group forms a special facet of the overall project – "a panel sample." Because of this feature of the study, we can explore how helping networks – kinds of helpers and their behaviors – develop from the onset of a problem to the continual coping with that concern over an extended time period.

Between March 1974 and August 1975 over 4,100 interviews were completed in the two waves of survey information used in the helping-network study. Each interview yielded over 1,000 items of information. 17 Black, 38 White and 4 racially mixed neighbors were included in the core study. Each interview was conducted in the home of the respondent and lasted 80 minutes on the average. Generally, the race of the interviewer and the respondent were matched. In most instances the second interview was conducted with the same interviewer.

The Aging and Retired Groups in the Survey

Throughout major portions of this report we will focus on individuals who have reached retirement age 65 – or report that they have recently entered retirement status. In terms of the total of 2,500 families interviewed in the Detroit Metropolitan sample, we find that 15.7 percent of the sample has attained the age of 65 years or older. At the same time, a total of 277 individuals report that they have been retired for at least one year prior to their first interview in 1974.

The newly retired individuals represent those persons who report that they retired within one year of their first interview. In addition, a group of persons near retirement, those who report after their first interview that they retired, comprise an important group of 40 individuals. Altogether, then, 331 persons sampled have already retired by the time that they were interviewed in the spring and summer of 1974. An additional 40 persons report being retired between 1974 and the time of their reinterview in 1975. This comprised 14.8 percent of the total sample. These patterns of age and retirement are generally representative of the Detroit metropolitan area as a whole. Thus 13.1 percent are age 65 or over according to the 1970 census compared to 15.7 percent in the helping-network sample. (See Appendix Table II-1.)

What about the quality of the interviews? We find that there is a general pattern for the reported understanding of persons being interviewed to decline with age. Thus, when asked by the study staff "compared to other respondents you have interviewed in this study, how well did the respondent understand the questions in the interview?" the staff of professional interviewers reported that 30 percent of those in the under-age-60 group were above average in understanding compared to only 8 percent of those who are 70 years old or older. In terms of suspicion, "How suspicious did R seem to be about the study before the interview?" we find that 83 percent of those under age 60 were reported to be not at all suspicious compared to 69 percent of those who were 70 or older. There is a steady increase in suspiciousness about the study with age. (See Appendix Table II-2.)

The various basic categories we employ in subsequent analyses show some major differences in basic social characteristics. Thus, in terms of racial composition, all of the four groups are similar, with the exception of persons who have retired within the last year, where nearly two-thirds of this group are black respondents. Only one in four for those who have retired for a longer period of time and one in five of other respondents are black. (See Appendix Table II-3.) Of the persons retired for more than a year, 56 percent are male. Of those recently retired, 50 percent are male, and for individuals who are about to retire, 43 percent and for other respondents, 45 percent respectively are male. (See Appendix Table II-4).

In Table II-1, the relationship between the age of the individual and their retirement status is shown. Those retired for more than one year who are age 70 or older are only three out of ten of the people that have just retired within the last year. More than one out of five individuals who have been retired for more than a year are below the age of 65. This reflects a variety of circumstances, some of which were described painfully by the respondents themselves who were either unwilling to retire or, because of an illness or physical disability, were forced to do so. Nearly one-half of the individuals who have retired within the last year are below the age of 65.

As we move from individuals not near retirement age to those who have been retired for more than a year, there is a steady increase in the proportion of people who are living in single-person households. However, the differences are not large between those on the verge of retirement and those who have been retired for a longer period of time. We find that only 7 percent of those who have been retired for more than a year are in a

TABLE II-1

Age Distribution by Retirement Status

	Retired more than 1 year before interview	Retired within the last year	To retire within 1 year after interview	Other persons inter- viewed
Age 70 or older	49%	22%	3%	3%
Age 65-69	29	34	0	2
Age 60-64	11	32	28	4
Under age 60	11	12	69	91
TOTAL	100% (N=277)[*]	100% (N=054)[*]	100% (N=040)[*]	100% (N=2103)[*]

NOTE TO THE READER: The N values shown are basically those which occur in all subsequent tables where the 4 analysis subgroups are presented. In these subsequent tables, the N sizes will not be shown.

TABLE II-2

Total Number of Persons Living in the Household

	Retired more than 1 year before interview	Retired within the last year	To retire within 1 year after interview	Other persons inter-viewed
Alone	31%	26%	23%	12%
2 persons	50	52	40	22
3 persons	12	13	15	20
4 or more	7	9	22	48
TOTAL	100%	100%	100%	102%

TABLE II-3
Martial Status of Persons Interviewed

	Retired more than 1 year before interview	Retired within the last year	To retire within 1 year after interview	Other persons inter-viewed
Married	59%	59%	75%	75%
Widowed	34	39	23	9
Divorced or separated	4	2	3	11
Single	4	0	0	6
TOTAL	101%	100%	101%	101%

household composed of four or more individuals. This is true for 22 percent of the households where a person is on the verge of retirement and nearly one out of two of other households. (See Table II-2.)

Three out of five of retired persons are married, compared to three out of four of the remaining sample. More than one-third of those retired are widowed. (See Table II-3.)

In terms of economic patterns, we find that one out of ten households of persons who have retired for more than a year contains a gainfully employed individual. Not surprisingly, this contrasts with 98 percent of those who are on the verge of retirement and 87 percent of other respondents not approaching the status. (See Appendix Table II-5.) Reported income shows that four out of five persons retired for more than a year have total family income of less than $10,000. This is similar also for persons who have recently retired. The figures exactly reverse themselves for those individuals on the verge of retirement where 81 percent report their income to be $10,000 or higher. We can clearly see the sudden shift in income that is reflected often within a very short period of one year or less. (See Table II-4.)

Not surprisingly the sources of income, among the retirees center on social security and pensions. Ninety-six percent of those retired for more than a year and 5 percent of those retired within the year depend on these sources of income. Interest and dividends, along with rental property income are reported by a majority of persons retired for more than a year. Those individuals who will retire within the year report wages in one out of four cases. Those who are near the age of retirement are most likely to report interest in dividend income, as well as to have a high proportion of persons reporting rent from property. (See table II-5.)

During the time interviews were conducted, Detroit and its metropolitan area experiencing were a severe economic "adjustment" because of a combination of the general economic slowdown and, particularly, the oil embargo which occurred in the fall of 1973. Effects continued for the next year in terms of high unemployment and weakened economic climate in Michigan. In view of this depressive economic situation, we asked individuals what sorts of sacrifices they had to make. (These

TABLE II-4

Family Income Reported by Respondent

	Retired more than 1 year before interview	Retired within the last year	To retire within 1 year after interview	Other persons interviewed
Under $3,000	14%	39%	0%	4%
$3,000-5,999	40	29	8	8
$6,000-9,999	26	10	11	10
$10,000-14,999	11	14	19	29
$15,000-19,999	5	2	16	21
$20,000-24,999	4	2	19	16
$25,000 or more	1	4	27	12
TOTAL	101%	100%	100%	100%

TABLE II-5

Reported Sources of Family Income of Respondent*

	Retired more than 1 year before interview	Retired within the last year	To retire within 1 year after interview	Other persons inter- viewed
Social security or pensions	96%	85%	15%	13%
Interest, dividends, trust funds, or royalties	40	24	58	35
Wages and salaries	17	26	98	90
Rent from property owned or from roomers & boarders	13	7	15	7
Other government aid, VA benefits, etc.	6	0	5	5
Public assistance or welfare	2	4	0	3
Alimony, regular contributions from family and others	2	2	3	3
Aid to Dependent Children	0	0	0	4

*

Percentages add to more than 100% since more than one source can be mentioned.

questions were asked in the follow-up 1975 interview.) Essentially, we can compare individuals who have retired very recently, those who have been retired for about a year or so, and those who have been retired for a longer period of time.

"Using up savings," "cutting back on vacations" and "being able to save less" are reported frequently by the individuals who have been retired for a year or so. This same group also reports they "go out less to shows and restaurants," and have "cut back on clothing," as well as "trying to economize food bills." Persons who retired before the first interview in 1974 do not report these kinds of sacrifices as frequently. This is reflective of the fact that, in general, they have a lower rate of such activities. Individuals who just recently retired, that is, in the midst of the economic turn-down, report their savings cut back and the fact of having to do more household and laundry work on their own, such as house painting and house repairs. (See Appendix Table II-6.)

Residency Stability of the Sample

The most basic focus of this report from the helping network study is the role of the residential setting – the neighborhood and community factors which might influence the well-being and the helping patterns of retired and aging individuals. The locality stability of the sample categories is reflected in the fact that about half of those who have been retired for more than a year at the time of their first interview report that they have lived in the same city for twenty years or more. Slightly over a third of those who have retired within the last year report that extent of longevity in their present municipality. Those on the verge of retirement show close to one-half living in their present community for at least twenty years. This contrast, with only 15 percent with this longevity of residence among other individuals in the survey.

Half of non-seniors and non-retired report that they have lived in the same city for five years or less. This is true in only one out of five instances, for the long-retired and for those who have retired within the last year.

The most stable residential groups, though, are those on the verge of retirement. Here, only 6 percent report that they have lived in their present community for five years or less. (See Appendix table II-7.)

In contrast to the very long period of time people report residing in the same city, living at the same address is concentrated at the ten to twenty year range. Recent retirees are more likely than those retired more than one year to be at their present address less than ten years. While only 6 percent of those on the verge of retirement report that they have lived at their present address for five years or less, 28 percent of those not near retirement report this pattern of relatively recent household movement. (See Table II-6.)

The overwhelming pattern characteristic of the Detroit metropolitan area is the detached single-family residence. Thus, 77 percent of those retired at least a year live in this kind of housing, with 70 percent of those who have recently retired so indicating. The highest level of single-family residents 95 percent – are among those individuals on the verge of retirement. Apartment dwelling, while growing substantially in terms of condominiums and other patterns, recently is still a fairly typical pattern. It increases from 0 percent for those near retirement to 8 and 10 percent respectively for those recently retired and retired for a longer period. (See Table II-7).

We can utilize descriptions of the age, the interior upkeep, the cleanliness of the household and the exterior yard and sidewalk condition of the residence as reported by the interviewer as a way of describing the quality of the environment of respondents. When we examine such patterns, we find that retired individuals are less likely to be in a household that is under twenty-five years old, as estimated by the interviewer. This is especially true of the group that has retired within the last year. Least likely to live in such structures are those who are not near retirement. Thus, we have a clear pattern of older residential settings being those in which retirees are characteristically located. (See Table II-8).

What about the conditions reported by the interviewer in terms of upkeep? Here we see a quite different pattern, particularly for those who have recently retired where 78 percent are reported to show an interior that

TABLE II-6

Length Time of Person Has Lived at Present Address

	Retired more than 1 year before interview	Retired within the last year	To retire within 1 year after interview	Other persons inter- viewed
2 years or less	5%	2%	3%	13%
3 to 5 years	5	9	3	15
5+ to 9 years	7	13	5	15
10+ to 19 years	66	69	68	51
20 years or more	16	7	23	7
TOTAL	99%	100%	102%	101%

TABLE II-7

Type of Housing Respondent Lives In

	Retired more than 1 year before interview	Retired within the last year	To retire within 1 year after interview	Other persons inter- viewed
Detached single-family residence	77%	70%	95%	80%
Two-family structure (side by side or two story)	9	15	5	7
Apartment (all types)	10	8	0	9
Row house (or town house structure)	3	8	0	4
Trailer	1	0	0	1
TOTAL	100%	101%	100%	101%

TABLE II-8

Physical Condition of Respondents' Residences

	Age[*] (more than 25 years old)	Interior[#] (very well)	Exterior[@] (very well)
Retired more than 1 year before interview	56%	69%	63%
Retired within the last year	70%+	78%+	69%+
To retire within 1 year after interview	48%	68%	63%
Other persons interviewed	34%	65%	57%

[*]

Three categories were provided: 1) more than 25 years old; 2) 5 to 25 years old, and 3) less than 5 years old.

[#]

Four categories were provided: 1) very well, 2) mixed--could us a paint job, 3) poorly--needs painting and minor repairs, 4) very poorly--dilapidated.

[@]

"How well kept up and cared for are the yards and/or sidewalks in front of the structure?" Categories were: 1) very well, fairly well, poorly, and very poorly.

is kept up "very well." The situation for the longer-term retirees is similar to that for other individuals in the survey.

When we look at responses to a question about plans to move, we find, not surprisingly, that seniors and those who are retired seldom report desire to move. Thus, 92 percent of those retired for more than a year say they have no plans to move as contrasted with 68 percent of those who are not near retirement age. (See Appendix Table II-8.)

Summary

In this brief description of the major sample stoups, we have found some generally predictable patterns. Retirees show restricted income, limited family size, and a high degree of residential stability. It is important to recognize that the high dependency that seniors have on their immediate residential setting is something which may be particularly important when that setting becomes threatened with decline or deterioration.

In spite of the often friendly and warm reception that interviewers received from seniors and retirees, the degree of fear or resistance to the survey was high among persons of advanced age. While this is consistent, with a number of other survey patterns, it also points out the fact that one should be cautious in interpreting data that may arise from interviews in which the degree of concern about the value of the study, as well as the need to have someone come to the house to take opinions and attitudes is a factor that may well bias our results or those of any study of retirees and seniors. While we have no data directly suggesting such a bias, it is clear, as we shall see in subsequent analyses of the number of problems reported by the seniors and retirees, that the lower level that we note may, in part, reflect the verbal exchange situation in which the information was gathered.

Now let us turn to the commonly experienced concerns that were the focus of the core helping-network study and the particular ways in which seniors and retirees report coping with these problems.

CHAPTER III

PROBLEM LOAD: A SUMMARY VIEW

This family has gone through two serious crises recently. First, they were forced out of their home on threat of death. The first assault was on the way to work and the man would wait for her each morning so that she had to take a different route each day to avoid him. Then the rock throwing – all back windows of the house were broken and one rock just missed her back. Then shooting at them in their house. They had to sell out and move in two weeks. This happened in 1971, but is still a nightmare to them. They lost their property which they owned and had kept up in very good repair.

At this time the husband's back was giving him a lot of trouble. They were going to the company doctor who said it was arthritis and nothing could be done. In desperation, after trying St. John's Doctor's Hospital, and private physicians, they went to Ford Hospital where he was immediately admitted for surgery. During the husband's stay at Ford Hospital, the wife also had to have minor surgery and was off work for four weeks. They are very happy where they are now living, but any signs of decay raise up the old nightmare. The feeble-minded son is a very minor concern to them with what else they've been through. A forced retirement of spouse will send them back to Tennessee where they will become home-owners again. The fear of personal danger is still so great, it probably will not leave them as long as they are in Detroit. Since the police offered them no help when their lives were threatened, this is probably the last resource they would go to. For the fear here is another unreported police statistic.

Interviewer Thumb-nail Sketches

Let us now focus on the various sources of help-seeking that arise because the individual is confronted with a range of threats to his quality of life or where he wishes to reach out in order to improve the conditions of his social environment. In the major helping-network study there were a variety of questions that were asked that elicited answers about concern and problems that were facing people.

One of the general open-ended questions that we asked individuals was the following: "What are some of the major problems confronting people in this community?" This general inquiry elicited a wide variety of statements, ranging, of course, from the economic and energy and inflation problems confronting people to the crime situation and family roles, moral issues, education and a wide variety of other specific topics. When these questions were put to the persons in the various groups that we have focused on, it is worth noting that a somewhat less frequent mention of problems occurred both for those who have been retired a longer period of time and those who were not approaching retirement. Thus, the individuals who were near the point of retirement report a greater multiplicity of problems. (See Appendix Table III-1.)

In Table III-1 results are shown in regard to the nature of perceived problems which appear to have a personal effect on the individual or were related to the family, to the neighborhood or to the community in which the person resided. Persons recently retired are more likely to have their problems placed within a personal context in that they do effect them. Only 15 percent of the problems were coded as not personally affecting the respondent who had only been retired a year or so, in contrast to 26 percent of those who had been retired for at least one year.

TABLE III-1

"How Has this (Problem) Affected You or Your Family?"

	Retired more than 1 year before interview	Retired within the last year	To retire within 1 year after interview	Other persons inter- viewed
R says problem not affected self or family	26%	15%-	24%	26%
R describes how problem has affected him/her personally	29	36+	26	27
R describes how problem has affected his/her family	14	13	23+	19
R describes how problem has affected his/her neighborhood	15	24+	9-	9
R describes how problem has affected his/her community	7	4-	9	9
R describes how problem has affected him/her in other ways	8	8	10	10
TOTAL	99%	100%	101%	100%

Overall, however, retirees compared to others did not show a major difference in terms of whether problems were personally affecting them or not. There is, however, some tendency for individuals who are retired to focus on the neighborhood as an arena of problem discussion. This reaches its height for those who have just recently retired. While there are some differences that we have noted, overall our data do not support this kind of view of seniors or retirees as less involved with the problems of the world.

Those who have been retired for more than a year or so were far more likely to be able to think of a second or third problem beyond the first one that they mentioned, compared to those who are newly retired. We note that individuals who are most likely to report the greatest multiplicity of problems are those who are at the point at which retirement will occur shortly.

Life Crises

The Holmes and Rahe scale has been increasingly viewed as a reliable and sensitive measure of the potential for problems to be stressful. In the present survey, we selected a subset of items from the larger scale (a total of fourteen problems). We asked individuals to indicate whether they had experienced any of these in the last year or so. Table III-3 describes the frequency with which each of these various kinds of problems was reported. Most common, of course, was personal injury, where we find that three out of ten individuals reported such an experience within the past year. However, the frequency does not appear to be related to retirement status or age. At the same time we also note that the total number of such problems experienced (See Appendix table III-2) does show a significant difference in terms of those who have been retired for at least a year versus other respondents.

While retirement itself was one of the Holmes and Rahe life crises, if we ignore this and look at those persons who have experienced at least one other life crisis – a total of two or more – we find: only 15 percent of the persons who have retired for more than a year report more life events, compared to 43 percent for those who have retired within the last year and 33 percent of respondents not nearing retirement.

Thus, the implication would be that the Holmes and Rahe scale being used by many researchers (in this instance, to measure sources of stress) reflects the facts that a person who is recently retired may score higher, and the person who has been long retired may score lower than other groups. This may not accurately reflect a pattern which defines the total social environment within which the individual must function. However, it does suggest that such scales have to be carefully evaluated when employed on groups with differing age and retirement statuses.

TABLE III-2

**List of "Life Crises" Drawn from the Holmes and Rahe Scale
(Reported "in the last year")**

	Retired more than 1 year before interview	Retired within the last year	To retire within 1 year after interview	Other persons inter- viewed
Personal injury or serious illness	29%	30%	33%	28%
Death of a close family member	22	13-	23	18
Change of job	1	2	5	15
Began or ended school or job training	1	2	5	13
Spouse began or stopped work	1	2	3	13
New person added to the household	5	9	5	9
Been the victim of a crime	5	7	13	9
Child has left the household	2	2	8	7
Divorce	1	0	0	3
Death of Spouse	3	7	3	2
Marital separation	0	2	3	2
Fired from job	0	2	3	2
Been arrested	1	0	0	1
Retired	0	0	0	0

The "Recent Concerns"

The essential focus of problem coping in the helping-network study is a set of nine "recent concerns" which were developed after extensive pretesting at the beginning of the overall study. Those problems which deal with neighborhood, family and work are not randomly distributed by age or retirement status. Clearly, as individuals enter such life situations, their experiencing of these "recent concerns" tends to decline. This is reflected, as we see in Table III-3, in terms of people "wanting to get a completely different job." This declined precipitously for respondents approaching retirement status.

There are several problems which show a fairly similar frequency in the four analysis categories. First of all, we see that a feeling of "not being able to get going" is experienced within the last month by 13 percent of those who have recently retired; and by 15 percent of those retired for a year or longer. This same problem is least likely to be reported by those on the verge of retirement per se. At the same time, "wanting to move" because of crime is reported more by individuals on the verge of retirement versus those already retired. Neighborhood crime concerns show general uniformity by age level; the lowest reported level is 15 percent by those who have been retired for more than a year, and the highest shared by those retiring recently or about to retire – 21 percent. Not surprisingly, those about to retire are highest in currently "thinking how it would be to retire." Half report doing so in the "last month or so."

TABLE III-3

Recent Concern Problem Load By Respondent Age

	Percent with one or more recent concerns	Mean number of recent concerns
Under age 30	84%	2.4
Age 30-39	75%	1.8
Age 40-49	80%	1.8
Age 50-59	72%	1.4
Age 60-69	49%	0.8
Age 70 or older	26%	0.3

Clearly the recent concern list of problems is subject to the specificity of life stages in terms of the job and educational topics. However, neighborhood and mood problems may be seen as fairly "status free" problems – not sharply influenced by age or retirement per se.

Follow-up Survey and Problem Experience

The same series of "recent concern" questions were repeated in the follow-up 1975 interviews. There was a high degree of correlation in what problems were reported for both years of the survey – an average of 55 percent – when we look at those individuals who, in the first interview were about to retire and, in the second interview had just done so. We find there are three problems which appear to increase at the outset of retirement: "wanting to get a completely different job," "wanting to go back to school" and "feeling blue." All of these show an increase in 1975 over the rate reported in 1974 for those individuals who had not yet retired at the time of the first interview. Yet this group is less likely to report that they want to move from their neighborhood because of crime after, compared to before, retirement.

We find that 36 percent of those who have been retired for at least a year have experienced one or more of the recent concerns, compared to 77 percent of those who are not near retirement status. The other groups fall at intervals between. Thus, having a recent concern decreases as one enters retirement status and the longer one has remained in that status. The contrast is indeed a sharp one when one sees that those not entering retirement status are, in one out of two instances, to report three or more such concerns, while this occurs in only 13 percent of the cases for individuals who have been retired for a year or more.

As age increases, recent concerns drop from the high point for those under age 30, where there is an average of 2.4 problems per person, to 0.3 for those who have attained age 70.

One of the most basic functions of the study was to relate the number of problems and the kind of help people receive to the level of self-reported stress. Here an index, made up of three subscales, was constructed (see Appendix B) in which a series of individual questions dealing with help, feeling of depression, and reported psychosomatic symptomology all were combined to form a "risk to well-being score" (RISK). The index has a score range of 0 to 62 with the mean being 12.5 for persons 65 or older.[4]

In Chart III-1 we trace the percent of persons above the mean based on number of recent concerns and life crises. The chart depicts those who are 65 or older. For life crises as well as the recent concerns we note a steady linear increase in the RISK score. The correlation for concerns (gamma of +.40) is stronger than that of life crises (gamma of +.15). As we found in the overall study, then, the index of recent concerns is a very useful way to measure the potential of stress (RISK) as people face a range of threats to their social environment. These "concerns" and a sense of need to seek solutions or help complement the problems of several social ties which are described in the Holmes and Rahe scale.

CHART III-I

Number of Life Crises and Recent Concerns
in Relation to RISK Score for Seniors

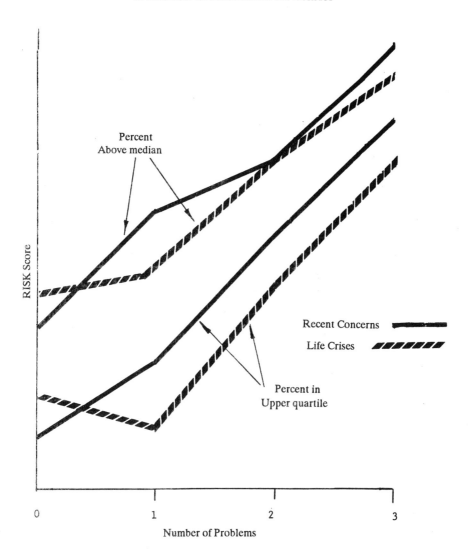

Summary

In this chapter we have described the sources of problems experienced by individuals, and we have noted that, for those who are retired or who are approaching retirement, there are some important differences in the degree to which problems are experienced. The number of Holmes and Rahe life crises is lowest for those persons who are retired for at least a year, but was his best for whose who have just entered upon the retirement status. In looking at the differences, then, what we see is that the experiencing of life events, while it is important, shows a very different pattern than that for recent concerns. Newly retired individuals, by the very fact of retirement itself, as well as other related life crises, show increased problem load.

"Life crisis" helping and social support is needed to adjust to the sudden change of status; the severing of a valued tie of a loved one or a work setting or other meaningful sources of social role performance. "Recent Concerns" reflect conditions of the person's environment with which they are dissatisfied. That is to say, they are not simply the absence of a condition, but the qualitative state of their life-style. Here we are referring, of course, to the problems that may arise in the neighborhood as well as to some extent in family relations and in one's general outlook on life. To the extent that one is feeling blue or is worried about crime in the neighborhood, the likelihood that one can do anything about such a problem may be a source of great anxiety and it is partly a matter of the use of resources that can make those problems less disturbing, of shorter duration perhaps, or that concrete actions in particular might be taken about them.

By contrast, the recent concern list seems to decline sharply. This is, to a major degree, a function of its composition: it focuses on employment and on the possibility of changing one's life in terms of schooling or retraining. But this measurement issue has theoretical implications as well. This very fact in itself should be borne in mind when one considers the situation of the retiree. We suggest that the Holmes and Rahe life crises, precisely because they are involuntary – imposed disruptions in networks – are the kinds of problems in which the individual is relatively powerless to act in resolving them. By contrast, recent concerns tend to be those problems over which the individual has an influence by virtue of their motivation and desire to change their life. This distinction is an important one.

The problem load of "recent concerns" may be viewed as a stimulus to social interaction. As such, the more the individual has these concerns, the more likely he is to need the resources of others. It is precisely this kind of reaching out or networking that we shall devote extensive attention to in subsequent sections of the analysis. Let us now turn to the kinds of resources that people utilize when they do experience recent concerns and examine the patterns of helping networks which do or do not emerge.

CHAPTER IV

HELPING NETWORKS: ISOLATION AND INTEGRATION

A very self-sufficient person. Doesn't seem to need or want help. She takes care of all her own problems, never discussing them with anyone else. She really seemed rather free of any problems. She had a lovely apartment, very neat and well furnished. She was sewing when I arrived. She told me she was 75 although last year she reported her age as 70.

R. received my unannounced visit with great kindness. I think R. has some problems walking (it was cumbersome), but her spirit was active, interested in people and neighborhood. R. loves to work with people, but is also content when alone. She always finds something to do.

Her husband was quiet, but displayed kindness. He told me later the story as follows: Two years ago they got a letter to get food stamps. They drove to the office on an icy, snowy day. The building was over-crowded with all sorts of undesirable people on the floor, along the walls, everywhere. They finally reached a girl who told them that they were out of applications, but they could come back on such-and-such a day. They never went back.

Interviewer Thumbnail Sketches

In examining the numbers of helpers used and the kinds of helpers used we shall be able to literally "map" the network patterns that emerge. It should also be kept in mind that the kind of problems that we have chosen do not necessarily represent the sources of helping that individuals utilize in some totally random or representative fashion. Instead what we have seen is that the "recent concerns" are a set of stimuli which can be viewed as activating the helping networks of an individual. It is in this state of mobilization of networks that we can begin to examine their effectiveness as well as their structure.

In the survey interview the question asked was: "How many kinds of people have you talked to about this problem?" And here the range of helpers, a total of ten different kinds, would be mentioned. We note, first of all, that a high degree of social isolation from helping networks occurs for those persons who have been retired for an extended period of time. Here, clearly one out of four of such individuals with a recent concern reports that they do not use any helpers in dealing with the problem. Half report using only one helper. For those who recently retired, two-thirds report using multiple helping sources.

Those near retirement are most likely to be involved in multiple networks when they are dealing with recent concerns, averaging 2.7. In terms of a life-course analysis, individuals go through a period in which they gradually build networks to a high point of utilization and then continue to employ this set of resources early in their retirement. But the pattern is followed by an isolation from helping networks.

We find that half of the individuals who have been retired for at least a year use two or more different kinds of helpers when they cope with recent concerns. They are not limited to a single system.

Individuals who are nearing that status have built up a network where, in two out of five instances, they use four or more different kinds of helpers. This is the case for only about one in ten of those who have been retired for more than a year, and for only 4 percent of those who recently have retired.

The very precipitous decline in the range of helpers used between those on the verge of retirement and those who have retired is in the dense networks of four or more different helpers, a decline on the magnitude of ten-fold. In terms of averages, those retired for longer periods of time use 1.6 helpers per problem, compared to 2.7 for those who are on the verge of retirement.

Let us examine in more detail the isolation from helping networks that is reflected in the move between those who have just retired and those who are on the verge of retirement. For those who have been retired for at least a year there is an increase from 35 percent to 41 percent in problems being handled without at least one helper. For those who had retired one year before them in 1974 and who were re-interviewed one year later (now two years retired) the increase in isolation is far more marked, going from 16 percent to 28 percent -- a 75 percent increase in isolation. For those who, had not yet retired and were interviewed in 1974, only 9 percent of their problems were being handled without at least one helper. One year later, at the time of their retirement, this pattern has increased to 29 percent. A 222 percent increase. Thus, we clearly see the sharp decline in network utilization that occurs as one passes through the stage of retirement. Persons who are not nearing the retirement status tend to use networks increasingly over time, so that there is a decline from 38 percent in 1974 to 29 percent in 1975 in not using any type of helping networks.

As we noted in Chapter III, experiencing a recent concern in 1974 is highly correlated with doing so one year later--1975. We find that a major factor in the continual experiencing of "recent concerns" is the pattern of having talked to at least one helper about that problem. About 60 percent of those who report this problem talk to someone about it. Out of the 29 percent of the entire sample who said they were thinking about retirement, 19 percent indicate they have talked to at least one helper about it, while 10 percent say they have talked to no one (see Appendix Table A-1). By 1975, half of those reporting they think about retirement have talked to someone in the previous year when they first mentioned this recent concern. Only one in five persons who reported the problem in 1975 had not previously talked to someone about it (see Appendix Table A-2). In other words, already experiencing the problem *and* having talked to someone about it increases the probability of experiencing the concern at a subsequent time. Thus, of those saying they thought about retiring in 1974 and also talked to someone at that time, about 60 percent in 1975 report the continuation of this concern. Of those who had the same problem in 1974 but at that time spoke to no helpers about it, 48 percent report the same concern in 1975 (see Appendix Tables A-1 to A-3).

As we noted in Chapter I, the function of PAHNs (Problem-Anchored Helping Networks) is to also reinforce the experience. This may or may not be conducive to good mental health. Yet it is clear that the "contending with problems"--the motivation to sustain a recent concern is--linked to contact with, versus isolation from, helping networks.

Who is a Helper for Recent Concerns?

Now let us examine each particular kind of helper that an individuals uses. In Table IV-3 each of the ten kinds of helpers are shown, and the percentage of people in each of the four analysis categories who report using one of those helpers for a recent concern. There are some expected changes, such as, of course, a decline in the use of a coworker as a helper. This type of helper was used by 27 percent of those who were on the verge of retirement, but declines to only 4 percent after retirement. Following retirement there is also a decline in the use of formal helpers. This, in turn, is matched by decline in the use of the spouse as helper. It should be borne in mind that we are not speaking of persons who are widowed, but simply those who do have a spouse available and the extent to which they may use them for handling a recent concern.

The use of the friend as a helper reaches a high point for those individuals who are on the verge of retirement--52 percent of these individuals with a recent concern using this kind of a resource. However, with retirement, this declines and we see a clear pattern that both friend and relative helping drops by the time the individual has been retired for at least a year. Neighbor helping increases the first year of retirement and then declines. For those retired for more than one year, friends, neighbors and relatives provide co-equal helping resources.

The use of formal services for recent concerns is generally limited and reflects the fact that such problems tend to emphasize "low-invoked expertise" which has a greater likelihood of using only informal resources.

Yet, those persons who do retire are far less likely than other individuals to go to the formal system for help with recent concerns.

When asked about the use of various social agencies in the general context of any contact within the last year, we find that the utilization of agencies shows a pattern which is quite consistent with that of seeking formal helpers for recent concerns. Thus, nearly three out of four of those who have been retired for at least a year report no such agency contact. The newly retired show a virtually identical pattern. Those on the verge of retirement are the most likely group to use the listed service agencies in coping with recent concerns. For all groups, use of a hospital or clinic is the major one mentioned. Here the pre-retirement group is the highest user at 35 percent and the post-retirement group the lowest--23 percent (see Table IV-4).

When respondents were asked if they had a friend who works in a service agency, retirees are less likely to report using a clinic or hospital on the basis of having a friend working there than are other respondents. Those retired two years or longer are especially less tied to informal linkages to a health care provider. This is simply another indicator of the specification as to what a "decline of social integration" means for retired persons. It is interesting to speculate about the way in which the informal network may, because of its value, be a source of leading people to use formal agencies with a high degree of confidence (see Appendix Table IV-1).

Helping Networks by Sex and Race of Older Respondents

A comparison of respondents 65 and older using gender and race reveals highly established patterns. Overall, white women have the smallest helping networks in the sense that their total of helping across the various formal and informal resources gives the lowest sum. Blacks, in general, tend to be using neighbor helping more than whites. At the same time, black men use relative helping far more than do black women. White males use spouse helping as a resource twice as often as is the case for white married women. White men are also less likely to use friend helping than are white women. Black retirees of both sexes and white males use a doctor for help less than white women. Yet, white women are twice as likely to use police as white men; but black men use such helpers twice as often as black woman. In general, for both blacks and whites, men use friend helping less than women do.

The Situation of the Single-Person Household

Now we turn to a particular grouping of individuals who have been retired with a special situation of isolation not previously dealt with--namely that they are living by themselves. We have previously noted that, roughly one-third of our sample retired at least a year are in this situation. Do they compensate for the absence of a spouse or other helpers in ways that set them apart as a group?

Clearly the role of spouse is a significant loss with only 8 percent using a spouse if they live alone compared to 72 percent of retirees who do not live alone. We also see a decline in the use of relative helping from 42 to 26 percent. There is some evidence of a compensatory pattern to the extent that friend helping is the most frequently employed resource. Thirty-nine percent of those living alone use a friend for recent-concern helping, compared to 26 percent of retirees who do not live alone. Neighborhood helping also is high but not significantly higher than retirees who do not live alone.

A Note on Life Crisis Helping Networks

As part of the follow-up interview in 1975, details were obtained about the kinds of helpers used not only for recent concerns, but for those on the list of "life crises." Here we find that, in regard to professional helping, there is a significantly higher use of the physician by those persons who have been retired at least a year (57 percent) compared to (45 percent) those who have very recently retired and lower still for other respondents in the sample (38 percent).

Persons who are not near the age of retirement are more likely to have other kinds of life crises than health and this may explain the high use of the physician as we move from immediate retirement to longer-term retirement. However, if we look specifically at the situation of people who have been retired for about a year at the time of their interview, in general they show a very high use of formal helpers, specifically police and clergy (see Appendix Table IV-2).

The Evaluation of Helpers

Given the fact that the helper may be available and used, there is still the question of how that helper is evaluated. The interview contained a general assessment of the various types of helpers. We find that there is a clear pattern in which the spouse is viewed as increasingly helpful as we move from those not near retirement to those that have been in retirement for more than a year. There is a similar pattern of increase as we move from non-retirement into retirement status. In general, friend helping seemed to be particularly valuable for those who have just retired (see Appendix Table IV-3).

Let us now compare the helper as evaluated and the helper as used. Table IV-7 provides the pertinent comparison. We first note that the spouse is viewed increasingly as a missing and yet valued helper for "recent concerns." Thus, those who have been retired show a deficit: their use of spouse as helper is far less than their desire for such helping. Relative helping also shows this same pattern at retirement status. Friend helping (which is really seen as less valuable and used more before retirement) begins to balance out after retirement. Neighbor helping in general is seen to be somewhat less valuable than its usage might suggest. This does not seem to change consistently with retirement. Also, those who have been long retired seem to value the help of co-workers when it is no longer available.

We see that what is characteristic of the person who has been retired for at least a year is that spouse, kin and co-worker are seen as highest in their helping value, but are not utilized to the degree such a rating implies. A similar deficit occurs for the newly retired, although it is not quite as extensive and is particularly focused on spouse and relatives. For individuals who are not retired, there seems to be a more general use of helpers.

Well-Being and Helping Networks

How does the extent of isolation or the extensitivity of the helping network relate to the individual's well-being? Is there a positive correlation?

This is a complex question that we can analyze from several points of view. The group with the lowest risk score is, in fact, the individual on the verge of retirement, with a mean of 11.8 on the RISK score. Individuals with the highest RISK score are those who have recently retired--17.3 is the mean. Thus, scope of network--average number of helpers per problem--is correlated with well-being.

There were two additional measures of stress used in our study: 1) a self-report of whether a person has gone to a doctor for extra health appointments and 2) whether a person has gotten extra medicine "to help them relax." Individuals that are newly retired rank high on such measures. Respondents who have recently retired are more likely to report doing both of these things far more than are other respondents (see Table IV-9).

In Chart IV-I we have graphed the mean RISK score in terms of the number of recent concerns, the number of helpers used and the situation of having no helpers for the problem. There is a clear linear relationship between problem load and risk to well-being. Having no helpers is associated with a reinforcement of this pattern. However, after the second problem we begin to see the role of the number of helpers in moderating the risk curve. Thus, we have some evidence that a large network of helpers may be associated with the lowering of risk where the problem load is high. Isolation from helpers shows an exacerbation of risk to well-being of persons age 65 or older.

Summary

We have examined in this chapter the question of isolation from helping networks, the number of different types employed and the size of helping networks in coping with "recent concerns." Persons who have been retired for at least a year are much more likely to cope with the problems without help from other persons. There is also apparent a sharp and precipitous shift in the range of network contacts that the person nearing retirement has as compared with the person that has just entered that status. It might be suggested here that a kind of problem or stress level associated with a sudden major status transition becomes moderated over time. That is to say, individuals who "acclimate" themselves to retirement status begin to select those key helpers with whom they can develop effective ties. In this theory of "functional adjustment," the hypothesis offered is that the most stressful time will be that period immediately following retirement where the individual must adjust to a smaller social network.

Despite major stereotypes in our society, there appears to be no particular correlation between age and social isolation. The general myth of the elderly being isolated is one that needs to be more fully specified. What is the nature of this isolation? Our own findings suggest that there is indeed a very marked degree of isolation that occurs. Moreover, *this has more to do with problems that one experiences that are not crisis.*

When the individual is reaching out for help for "recent concerns" they may find that thee are helpers who are not available that they would find valuable to have. Thus, even though the co-worker, kin and spouse are often viewed as effective helpers, they are no longer available to the person who has been retired for an extended period of time. This pattern suggests that other helpers are used who may be less satisfactory in their role.

Finding alternative helpers is a major topic of analysis that we shall subsequently explore in greater detail. It is valid to suggest from our data that retirement status is not a single stage, but, rather, conforms to what is viewed as a two-step process. The individual who is recently retired begins to find a range of helpers the first year after retirement. Far from being isolated, they may, in fact, show an increase in reaching out and in the use of helping resources. Findings do indicate that this group is likely, when they do reach out, to not reach toward a formal helper for the kinds of concerns that we have discussed but may in fact use various resources of the community which are shared with the health professional. Ironically, it may well be, as our data suggest, that the use of medication increases in this first year as a way to cope with the stress or isolation that the individual may feel. But following this initial stage, there is a reversal which occurs.

We found that there was a sharp increase in neighbor helping following retirement. This may suggest that what happens is the individual simply turns to whoever is accessible, and that once that process has occurred, it would be difficult to see the individual building a steady or reliable relationship of mutual help or social support. The retired person who lives alone begins to turn to friends even more than other retirees. What happens if the neighbor is turned to but the friend is a preferred helper yet is not accessible? Does the individual become more selective? Is it possible, for example, that the kind of help must begin to shift? For the neighbor to take the place of the friend or the spouse in terms of a range of problem-coping responses, such change is critical. We now turn, then, to the question not simply of who is a helper, but *what kind of help* might be provided. There is a sense in which it is not simply the *size* of the network alone that is critical to well-being, but the *content* as well.

CHART IV-1

Number of Helpers, No helpers and Number of Recent
Concerns in Relation to Risk score
for Persons 65 or older

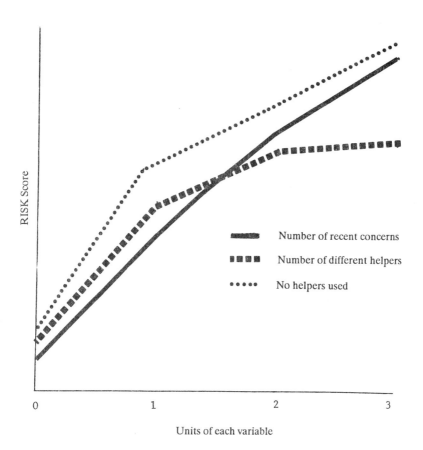

TABLE IV-1

**Number of Different Kinds of Helpers
For Retired and Non-retired Persons
1974 Baseline Sample**

	Retired more than 1 year prior interview	Retired within 1 year of interview	Retired in following year (1975)	Other Respondents
Did not use helpers for recent concerns	23%	8%	4%	14%
Used one kind of helper	25	25	34	24
2 kinds of helpers	31	25	19	23
3 kinds of helpers	11	38	3	17
4 kinds of helpers	6	4	15	11
5 or more kinds of helpers	3	0	26	12
TOTAL	99%	100%	101%	101%
	(N=277)	(N=59)	(N=40)	(N=2064)
Mean number of helpers per problem	1.6	2.1	2.7	2.0

TABLE IV-2

Selected Recent Concerns and Isolation from Helpers[*]

	Percent of of problems 1974	No helpers 1975	Percent change 1974-75
Retired more than 1 year before	35% (N = 135)	41% (N = 90)	+17%
Retired within the last year	16% (N = 032)	28% (N = 014)	+75%
To retire within 1 year after interview	9% (N = 023)	29% (N = 035)	+222%
Other persons interviewed	38% (N = 3459)	29% (N = 1671)	-24%

[*]

The problems included are: 1) feeling blue, 2) feeling it's no use trying, 3) suspicious people in the neighborhood, 4) thinking about going back to school, and 5) thinking about moving because of neighborhood crime.

TABLE IV-3

Type of Helper Used for "Recent Concerns"

	Retired more than 1 year before interview	Retired within the last year	To retire within 1 year after interview	Other persons inter- viewed
Spouse	44%-	39%-	70%	64%
Relative	28 -	59 +	48	38 -
Friend	28 -	41	52 +	44
Neighbor	28	41 +	25	27
Co-worker	1 -	4 -	27	23
Formal helpers	18 -	16 -	30 +	23
Doctor	6	5	15 +	8
Police	11	8	15	8
Councelor*	1	4	4	6
Clergy	1	8 +	11 +	4
Teacher	0	0	7 +	4
Sum of helpers	145%	200%	252%	219%

*

Counselor includes social worker, psychiatrist, and psychologist.

TABLE IV-4

Number of Human Service Agencies Contacted*

	Retired more than 1 year before interview	Retired within the last year	To retire within 1 year after interview	Other persons inter- viewed
None	72%	72%	57% –	61% –
One	21	23	30	26
Two or more	7	6	13	13
TOTAL	100%	101%	100%	100%
Used a clinic or hospital in the last year	26%	23%	35%	30%

*

Agencies included are: 1) local clinic or hospital, 2) state social service agency, 3) state or federal job-related agency, 4) county social service agency, 5) city social service agency, 6) legal service agency, 7) civil rights organization, 8) private psychologist or psychiatrist or 9) community mental health agency.

TABLE IV-5

**Sex and Race in Relation to Helping
Networks of Seniors
(Recent concerns)**

| | White | | Black | |
	Male	Female	Male	Female
Spouse	77%+	37%	52%	0%-
Relative	26	27	33	58+
Friend	26	37	24	37
Neighbor	26	30	38+	37+
Co-worker	3	3	0	5
Doctor	13+	3	0	0
Police	3	7	19+	10
Counselor*	0	0	0	10+
Clergy	0	3	0	5
Teacher	0	0	0	0
TOTAL	174%	147%	166%	162%

*

Includes social worker, psychiatrist, psychologist.

TABLE IV-6

**Helping Networks of Retired Persons Who Live
Alone Compared to Those who
Do Not**

	Lives Alone	Does not Live Alone
Spouse	8%	72%+
Relatives	26%	42%+
Friend	39%+	26%
Neighbor	3%	31%
Co-worker	3%	8%+
Formal helpers	21%	24%
Doctor	3%	5%
Police	14%	12%
Counselor*	0%	5%
Clergy	5%	5%
Teacher	0%	1%
TOTAL	153%	231%

*

Counselor includes social worker, psychiatrist, and
psychologist.

TABLE IV-7

**Informal Helpers Used Compared to How Helpful
Each is Perceived to Be**

	Retired more than 1 year before interview	Retired within the last year	To retire within 1 year after interview	Other persons inter-viewed
Spouse	-37%	-36%	- 4%	- 7%
Relative	-17%	-20%	+ 6%	+ 5%
Friend	+ 6%	- 2%	+24%	+19%
Neighbor	+ 7%	+16%	+ 9%	+14%
Co-worker	-25%	+ 4%	+ 4%	+ 7%
Total discrepancy	92%	78%	47%	52%
Net deficit	-56%	-30%	+39%	+38%

TABLE IV-8

**Risk to Well-being Score (RISK) in Relation
to Analysis Groups**

	Retired more than 1 year before interview	Retired within the last year	To retire within 1 year after interview	Other persons inter- viewed
Mean score	15.3	17.3 +	11.8-	15.0
Low quartile	25%	20%	28%	25%
High quartile	29%	33% +	20% -	28%
Percent above mean	48%	52%	45% -	51%

TABLE IV-9

**Recent Seeking of Professional
Special Medical Help for Stress**

	Retired more than 1 year before interview	Retired within the last year	To retire within 1 year after interview	Other persons inter-viewed
In the last several weeks have you made any extra doctor's appointments to take care of a health problem?	11%	19%	13%	13%
In the last several weeks have you gotten any extra medicines at the pharmacy or drug store to help you relax	12%	19%	8%	9%
TOTAL	23%	38%+	21%	22%

CHAPTER V

THE KIND OF HELP PROVIDED BY HELPERS

R. does house repairs for neighbors occasionally. There are lots of nice friendly people in the neighborhood. City services (garbage pick-up) could be a lot better.

R. has been helping an old lady across the street whose social security payments are so low she can't afford to buy meat or enough food. Her heat bills runs $57.00 a month. R. was so upset about this that she readily gave her own account numbers as their homes are similar and neighbor sits in darkness at night because of high cost of electricity.

R. is often called upon to cheer someone up. She goes out of her way to help people and mentioned several times "rolling so and so's hair." She mentioned she was widowed when her son was seven years old. She went to work at the Bomber Plant during World War II and raised and educated her son. As I was leaving she showed me her new "Living Bible," a phone number from a Baptist church you can call anytime and have them pray for you, and a Novena card a Catholic friend had given her.

Interviewer Thumbnail Sketches

Built into our metropolitan survey are measures that describe a set of six different types of help individuals could select if they talked with another person about a "recent concern." In effect, these responses provide a third-dimension to our analysis of networks, namely the size or number of problems, the numbers of different types of helpers used and the variety of helping behaviors that are provided. On this latter point, the behaviors are described as follows: just listening, asking questions, showing the person a new way to look at the problem, referring them to someone else or taking them to someone else, and finally taking action on the problem. By grouping the two responses of telling and taking to someone else under the category referral, we then utilize five basic forms of helping behavior.

If we look at those individuals who have been retired for a year or more, there are nearly half the helping behaviors available than to those who are not nearing retirement-- 2.7 per helper, compared to 1.4. Thus, there is a steady decline in the number of different kinds of helping behaviors available as one moves through the retirement status and on into old age. (See Table V-1.)

Through comparisons of helping over the one-year time from the first interview to the second, we see that those who have recently retired show a substantial increase in helping behaviors. The number of behaviors per problem per helper declines from 2.4 to 1.6 for those who pass through retirement from their first to second interview.

We find that "just listening" behavior is most characteristic of the help received for individuals who have recently retired. They are also more likely than others to receive help that deals with "showing a new way to look at a problem." In general, those who have just entered into retirement or who have been retired for over a year are more likely to get referral behaviors than are other respondents, but are given less than average direct-action helping. (See TABLE V-2)

As one enters retirement, we see that "listening" declines--from 46 percent of all helping behaviors to 41 percent. "Asking questions" increases slightly, and "showing a new way" nearly doubles in proportion to other helping behaviors. At the same time, "referral" and "action" helping tend to decline. Retirement is associated more with "social support" and behaviors which elicit direct change in the person's life or put them in contact with other helpers--"instrumental helping." (See Table V-3.)

If we now take into account the various kinds of helping, we find that there is a steady increase in "listening" as a behavior when one goes from the under-thirty group to higher age groupings up to the sixties. Thus "listening" declines after thirty--then increases in age--seventy or older group. At the same time, there is a decline in "asking questions" and "referral," and a steady decline from age thirty onward (where it is 39 percent of all helping transactions) in "taking action" helping. By age group seventry it is only 12 percent of all helping.

We find that those who are in the situation of being on the verge of retiring are far more likely to get "action helping" than those who are newly retired. At the same time, the "showing of a new way to look at problems" goes up once the retirement occurs and is similar to the pattern found for people who are not nearing retirement. (See Table V-4.)

There is also, for the person who crosses from pre-to post-retirement (1974-75) a decline in both referral and action help.

The pattern for crisis helping which was analyzed for the 1975 follow-up interview shows a difference in what kind of help for a crisis is offered, depending on retirement status. The referral and asking of questions pattern is particularly pronounced for those who have been retired for a year or two. Helping by asking questions declines as well. When all the behaviors which are not listening are added the proportion of listening to non-listening behavior for both crises and recent concerns goes up for the group that has retired: 74 percent of all transactions compared to 65 percent for those who have been retired a year or two. (See Table V-5.)

We have been measuring the kind of help received. But is that which is available really the type of help sought or not? Several questions were introduced into the study which attempted to look at the "reciprocity" issue, that is to say, whether the kind of help one received was the kind that one wanted. There were several measures utilized. One was a question asking: "What is the most helpful thing that a person experiencing the kinds of problems we have talked about can use?" Another way to put it was to ask

"Who is the most helpful kind of person--someone who does which of the following things?"

Among those who have been retired, nearly one out of five say they need no help. This reflects the fact that not seeking help among the persons who are of a retirement status may partly be a reflection of their view that they can do things without relying on others. Such attitudes are probably much more prevalent in this group than for those entering retirement where zero percent of the respondents said that they found nothing would be helpful. (See Table V-6.)

People who are of retirement status are less likely to see listening as the most helpful behavior. This is extremely significant in light of the fact that this is the same group that receives more listening than other groups. This same group--long-term retired persons--is more likely to say that "suggesting a solution" and "doing something" and "taking action" are considered the most helpful things. A quarter of the individuals who have been retired for more than a year choose such answers, compared to only 11 percent of those who are not nearing the retirement status. This pattern is retained in 1975 (See Appendix Table V-1).

The person who is just entering retirement, as well as the person who has had longer-term retirement, is most likely to find a deficit of active helping and a surfeit of listening helping. It appears to be particularly pronounced in terms of those who have just recently retired. Moreover, this group shows a significant deficit in terms of referral behavior. They want a lot more than they actually receive, or they consider referral behavior to be very desirable (See Table V-7).

Still another facet of the nexus of helping as reciprocative social involvement can be seen by the kind of helping that the respondent offers when they are turned to for help themselves. If we take as a general theoretical perspective the notion that "helping networks" are really valuable forms of social integration, precisely because the individual is able to provide the "grass-roots expertise" to another that they, in turn, can seek from "peers." It is precisely in this lack of status difference between helper and helpee--the absence of a formal professional status difference--that makes this particular form of social exchange distinct and significant.

We find a decline bay half between those not nearing retirement status, (where 26 percent had said that they were a recent helper), to only 13 percent for those who had been retired for more than a year. This latter group is clearly not as open to a reciprocal helping role as others in the sample. When we look at the particular kind of help that they offer when they do have the opportunity to help, we find differences based on retirement status. Those who are retired are less likely to say that they "asked questions" and that they "wanted action." They defined themselves as sympathetic listeners who often were able to cheerup the person that they spoke to. They could on occasion also sometimes take action. (See Table V-8.)

In general, "listening" help is more likely to be given than received by a relatively small margin for those who are retired for more than a year. "Asking questions" helping behavior tends to be most clearly reciprocated among those who have just retired or who are about to retire. "Action" helping and "referral" helping are both less likely to be obtained than given by persons who have been retired for more than a year. This sharp difference is also present in terms of those sampled who are not nearing retirement. Clearly, all sample catergories indicate they do not receive as much "action" helping as they would want. (See Table V-9.)

Risk Levels and Type of Helping

Aside from the particular form of help there is evidence of a relationship between the type of help provided and what is most effective. In the overall sample it was found that, "listening" help, not accompanied by other forms of helping, did not reduce the RISK score. The percent of those over 65 who have a RISK level in the upper one-quarter scored (20 or more) does vary with the type of help they received for recent concerns. Those who report no listening are somewhat less likely than those that receive no referral to have a high RISK score.

When "listening" help alone is considered, the level of high risk increases much more sharply than when all varieties of helping are considered. This pattern is even more sharply defined for the seniors in the study with more than two recent concerns. Thus, as problem load increases, the number of concerns increases the probability of a high RISK score; and "listening" behavior tends to be less salient in reducing stress than when either the number of helpers involved or the amount of helping behaviors beyond listening is considered.

CHART V-1

Problem Load, Helpers Used, Number of Listening Behaviors and
all forms of Helping in Relation to RISK score:
Persons 65 or older or under 65

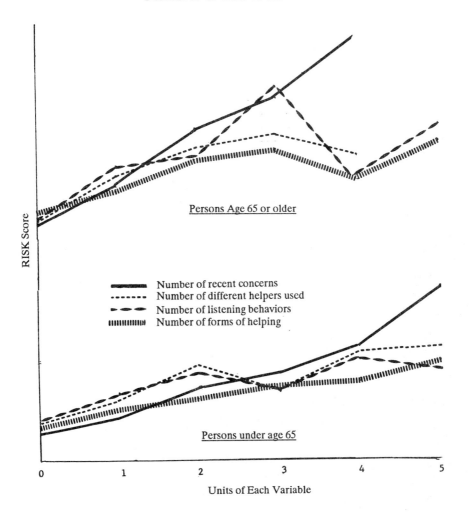

Persons Age 65 or older

Number of recent concerns
Number of different helpers used
Number of listening behaviors
Number of forms of helping

Persons under age 65

RISK Score

0　　　1　　　2　　　3　　　4　　　5

Units of Each Variable

Summary

This chapter has provided a way to examine helping in term of helps, and what kind of help is provided. We have found that there is a closer knitting together of the help wanted and the help received for those who have not entered into a retirement status. As we go beyond the point of retirement, we find that individuals are more likely to receive "listening" help to give "action" help and are less likely to give "referral" help and to give "action" help. The situation of a person retired for a year or longer reflects a looser fit between what is wanted in the way of helping and what the individual receives, and what, in turn, the individual may give back in the form of a reciprocated network.

Our findings suggest that retirement status restricts the effectiveness of networks to function because they limit the ability of the individual to reciprocate, to select the kind of help that they want and, in turn, to give the kind of help to others that they feel they would like to have themselves. Moreover, the fact that such patterns are likely to reflect a restricted reciprocity further underscores the implication of a number of different findings which social integration of the aging as a process not only of isolation from helping, but from mutual helping networks.

This theme, which we shall elaborate on in subsequent chapters, does indicate that it is not so much isolation per se, but the fact that when help is needed, it is less likely to be in the form that is desired. Seeking of help from individuals involves an assumption that there is a high probability that the kind of help wanted will not in fact be that which is granted to others.

"Matching" is less likely to be fulfilled when a person newly enters the retirement status or appears to remain in that status over a more extended time period. It is therefore in the discussion of networking possibilities that we must suggest not only the relative reduction in opportunities for entering into the helping relationships that accompanies aging and retirement, but that the satisfaction with such transactions and the possibility of maintaining them because of a continued give and take is therefore reduced.

Finally, in this chapter we reviewed data showing that the types of helpers and helping behaviors reported for recent concerns affected the RISK scope of seniors to the same extent as other sample respondents.

Volume of helping with a high problem level offers an even more sensitive barometer of well-being than for non-seniors.

TABLE V-1

Number of Helping Behaviors Per Problem
And its Change: 1974-75

	Average Number of helping behaviors (1974)	Average Number of helping behaviors (1975)	Amount of change	Percent change: 1974-75
Retired more than 1 year before interview	1.4	1.6	+0.2	+14%
Retired within the last year	1.8	2.8	+1.0	+56%
To retire within 1 year after interview	2.4	1.6	-0.8	-33%
Other persons interview	2.7	3.0	+0.3	+11%

TABLE V-2

Type of Help Provided for Recent Concerns

	Retired More than 1 year before interview	Retired within the last year	To Retire within 1 year after interview	Other persons inter- viewed
Listening	89%	95%	95%	90%
Asking questions	56%	33%−	72%+	67%+
Showing a new way to look at the problem	22%	41%−	26%	39%+
Referring	21%	33%+	26%	25%
Taking action	22%	9%−	34%+	31%+

TABLE V-3

Comparison of Type of Help Provided for Persons
Who Retired Between 1974 and 1975

	1974 helping pattern (Pre-retirement)	1975 helping pattern (Post-retirement)
Listening	46%	41%
Asking questions	31%	34%
Showing a new way to look at the problem	9%	16 +
Referring	5%	3%
	} 14%	} 9%
Taking action	9%	6%
TOTAL	100% (N = 54)	100% (N = 54)

TABLE V-4

Age of Respondent and Type of Helping for
Recent Concerns

	Listens	Asks Questions	Show New Way	Refers	Takes Action
Under 30	83%	68%+	40%+	35%+	39%
30-39	85	67+	38+	25	30
40-49	73	50−	31	17	23
50-59	79	57	28	14−	19−
60-69	78	47−	23−	14−	13−
70+	88+	50−	31	25	12−

TABLE V-5

Type of Help Provided for Life Crises

	Retired More than 1 year before interview	Retired within the last year	To Retire within 1 year after interview	Other persons inter- viewed
Listening	74%	65% −	74%	76%
Asking questions	47% −	63%	50%	60%
Showing a new way	17%	17%	19%	15%
Referring	13%	35%	9%	10%
Taking action	8%	0%	2%	8%

TABLE V-6

What is the Most Helpful Thing When You Go To a Person "with a concern like the ones we have ben talking about"

	Retired More than 1 year before interview	Retired within the last year	To Retire within 1 year after interview	Other persons inter-viewed
Someone who will listen	16% –	18% –	29% +	39% +
Someone who is sympathetic, concerned, understanding	11	0	14	6
Someone who gives me new ideas, helps me see alternatives	11	27 +	0	7
Someone who will discuss the problem thoroughly, thrashes it out	7	0	14	14
Gives moral support	7	9	14	3
Someone who gets to the core of the problem	0	0	14	3
Suggests a solution, takes action, shows me something to do about the problem	0	0	14	11
I solve my own problems without help	18 +	18 +	0	6
Other things	4	10	0	10
TOTAL	99%	100%	99%	99%

TABLE V-7

Match Between Help Received and Help Wanted

	Retired More than 1 year before interview		Retired within the last year		To Retire within 1 year after interview		Other persons inter- viewed	
	get	want	get	want	get	want	get	want
Listening (1974)	47%	16%	57%	18%	46%	29%	45%	39%
	+31		+39		+17		+6	
Action and referral (1974)	8	25	2	18	9	14	7	11
	−17		−16		−5		−4	
Total discrepancy	48%		55%		22%		10%	
Listening (1975)	47%	25%	43%	39%	41%	55%	46%	47%
	+22		+4		−14		−1	
Action and referral (1974)	16	19	24	15	23	8	19	18
	−3		+9		+15		+1	
Total discrepancy	25%		13%		29%		2%	

92

TABLE V-8

Kind of Help that the Person Would Give[*]
If asked to be a Helper

	Retired More than 1 year before interview	Retired within the last year	To Retire within 1 year after interview	Other persons inter-viewed
Just listen to them talk it all out	88%	94%	87%	88%
Suggest ways to take action on the problem	78	81	93+	84
Tell them who else they ought to see for help	76–	75–	85+	84+
Ask them questions so they can get a better handle on the problem	75–	75–	82	82
Be sympathetic, but not try to give any advice	71+	50–	55–	65+
Joke and kid and try to cheer them up	60	63	64	61
Take them to someone who can take action	55	56	50	55
"Has a situation like this come up lately – in the past week or two?"	13%–	19%	18%	26%+

[*]The exact question is: "Suppose someone in the neighborhood, or a friend, a relative or someone you know at work tells you they are feeling pretty badly about their life and the problems they are dealing with. Which of the things on this list is the best way you know of helping them out?"

TABLE V-9

Match Between Type of Help Received and Type of Help Given

	Retired More than 1 year before interview		Retired within the last year		To Retire within 1 year after interview		Other persons inter-viewed	
	get	give	get	give	get	give	get	give
Listening	75%	88%	100%	94%	94%	87%	91%	88%
		13%		6%		3%		3%
Asking questions	64	75	70	75	80	82	72	82
		11		5		2		10
Referring	21	76	41	75	16	85	29	84
		55		34		69		55
Taking action	14	55	27	56	26	50	32	55
		41		29		24		23
Total discrepancy	120%		74%		98%		91%	

CHAPTER VI

NEIGHBORING AND NEIGHBOR HELPING

Her apartment was very neat and clean, modern, furnished. She was not very sociable. She liked her apartment, but not the people who lived there. "I love my apartment. It's just nice. I need some furniture, but I don't care. I just like it here. Where can I go, honey? It's cozy here. The people gossip a lot, but I don't bother with anyone. I mind my own business. They all think I'm strange and they don't understand me.

R. says that the neighbors, "aren't no help at all." When young men broke into her house and tried to kill her, no one [of the neighbors] knew anything. The neighbors were afraid to talk. The police came, but didn't do anything about the crime. She doesn't go out too much now since she's crippled, but some of the members still come and visit her. The neighborhood club has gotten a free ride for the seniors. This neighborhood ride will take seniors to cash their checks and bring them back because so many of the seniors get robbed of so much of their little money.

Interviewer Thumbnail Sketches

We find a great deal of evidence regarding the importance of neighborhood in the lives of seniors and retired persons. Persons who have been retired for a year stressed neighborhood as the focus of their concerns over on me. Those retired for a longer period of time also saw crime in the neighborhood as a more important problem than did individuals who were not retired. A number of questions in the survey dealt with perceptions as well as patterns of help-seeking for various kinds of problems. Those newly retired are far less likely to feel that the neighborhood is a "good place to live" than other respondents. Partially, this reflects the high proportion of black residents in this particular group of retirees. (Appendix Table VI-1). When such feelings about the neighborhood are correlated, with the self-reported well-being we do find a fairly consistent pattern. As one moves from viewing the neighborhood as "good" to viewing it as "very poor," the RISK score steadily increases (See Chart VI-1).

Past research of the author indicates that neighborhoods must be viewed from two perspectives: the subjective, perceived qualities, and the objective physical context. On this latter point, the judgement of the interviewers in regard to the quality of the services and condition of streets, lighting and other accoutrements of the neighborhood becomes a useful indicator. Persons nearing retirement and who have just retired are at least likely to be living in neighborhoods where public facilities are rated as "excellent." (See Appendix Table VI-2.)

As noted in Chapter II, the interviewer was also asked to estimate the age of housing of those persons interviewed as well as to describe the general upkeep of the interior and exterior of that dwelling. One of the ways to use this information is to see how congruent the pattern reported for seniors and retirees is in comparison with their neighborhood. In regard to estimated age, 56 percent of those persons retired for more than a year are living in dwellings that are estimated to be twenty-five years or older, compared with 51 percent for their neighbors. For persons who have been retired for more than a year, 19 percent are rated as having interior upkeep that is "very good," compared to 10 percent for their neighbors. In regard to exterior upkeep, persons who have been retired for a year or less are 21 percent more likely to have that condition reported as "very good," compared to their neighbors. The differential for those persons not nearing retirement is only 6 percent. (See Appendix Table VI-3.)

CHART VI-1

Attitude about the Neighborhood as a Place to Live in Relation
to RISK score for Persons age 65 or older

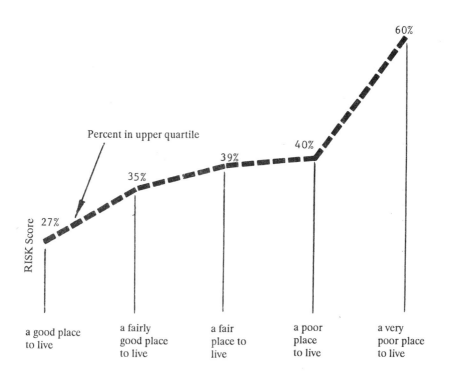

Perceived Neighborhood Size

We asked individuals to describe what they considered their neighborhood to be. The specific question was: "When you think of the area you consider your neighborhood, what comes to mind?" Several alternatives were presented, the first of which we may call the concept of the "micro neighborhood," that is, "people living right nearby (across the street or next door.)" This smallest concept of neighborhood is one which is most frequently selected by individuals who are newly retired. Forty-two percent of this group describe their neighborhood using this small-scale category. Individuals who are least likely to use this unit are persons who are not yet retired but who will do so within the next year: only 13 percent choose this "micro" level of neighborhood. (See Table VI-1).

Overall, the definition of neighborhood as "people on my block," is the most frequently selected unit. There is some tendency for people nearing retirement or who have already retired to select this unit, more than other respondents.

Smaller units of neighborhood, such as the block or less are chosen in four out of five instances by those who have recently retired. Sixty percent of those retired for a longer period of time choose such a smaller unit. Larger definitions of neighborhood, such as, "people within walking distance" are least likely to be chosen by the newly retired. Persons who have been retired for more than a year choose a "larger than walking distance" neighborhood 15 percent of the time. This is chosen by those newly retired only 6 percent of the time, in contrast to 21 percent for persons who are about to retire as well as those not nearing retirement status.

Social Contacts with Neighbors

Actual contact with neighbors was measured by asking people how often they visited with neighbors "on this block or in this general area," that is, "getting together at your home or theirs." We find that there is no sharp difference in terms of the various groupings of retirement and non-retirement in the frequency of visiting patterns. Turning to the question of the number of friends in the neighborhood, we find that the common pattern, with the exception of the newly retired, is that one in four individuals say they have no close friends. While it is true that those who are on the verge of retirement are more likely to report ten or more close friends in the neighborhood, it is also true that those who have been retired for longer than a year have at least ten friends or more 14 percent of the time in contrast to those newly retired where the figure is 6 percent. (See Table VI-2).

Turning to Neighbors in the Energy Crisis

The question that came up in regard to the energy crisis at the time of our interview was whether or not individuals were spending more time with their neighbors because of energy shortages. We find that all groups tended to report some increase in neighboring, but that this was especially evident for those who were newly retired. There was also some tendency for those on the verge of retirement to show a higher increased frequency due to the energy situation. Thus, 34 percent of those on the verge of retirement reported seeing neighbors more often (at least once a week) and 32 percent of those newly retired, contrasted with 22 percent of the persons retired for a longer period of time and 23 percent for those not approaching retirement. (See Appendix Table VI-3)

Neighboring and the Well-Being of Seniors

Let us now correlate several neighborhood variables with RISK. Chart VI-2 shows that the condition of public facilities as well as perceived size of neighborhood both affect the RISK score significantly. We see that what occurs is that the risk to well-being tends to remain similar until general facilities are reported to be less than good. In regard to, the perceived size of neighborhood, those seniors who choose the small-scale micro-neighborhood tends to be associated with the highest above mean RISK scores. This declines through the "block" definition to the "walking distance" unit which is associated with the lowest RISK score among individuals age 65 or older. Thus, overall, where the general facilities of the neighborhood are reported by the interviewers to be at least "good" and the senior chooses a walking-distance-size neighborhood, we find the least likely above average RISK to well-being score.

The correlation between social contacts with neighbors and well-being shows a curve linear pattern. Those individuals who are least likely to be above the mean level in RISK are seniors who report that they are in touch with their neighbors twice a month. Contact which is more frequent or less frequent is associated with a greater probability of giving an above mean RISK score. (See Chart VI-3.)

Organizational Links to Neighbors

Let us now turn to the secondary participation level of individuals in the neighborhood. Here we are dealing with a measure of the extent to which people belong to voluntary associations where they see their neighbors. Persons retired for more than a year are least likely to belong to organizations where neighbors also belong. Individuals nearing retirement are the group most likely to do so. (See Table VI-3).

Membership in local neighborhood associations such as block clubs is 23 percent for those who recently retired, contrasted with 16 percent of those who have been retired for more than a year. The kinds of groups that are the most typical places where neighbors are seen include church membership, and this is particularly the case for those on the verge of retirement or who have just retired. There are several kinds of organizations where neighbors are seen by those persons nearing retirement. These include church-connected groups, fraternal and veterans organizations, civic groups, youth groups, sports teams, social actions and charitable organizations. (See Appendix Table VI-4.)

When we then compare the extent to which neighbors will be seen at association meetings, we find some significant differentials based on retirement. For 6 of the 16 different kinds of groups a majority of those retired for more than a year report they see neighbors. By contrast, this is true for 11 of the 16 groups where persons were not nearing retirement. In fact, the entrance into retirement status seems to be the critical dividing point: 69 percent of those on the verge of retirement are active in groups in which there are neighbor contacts. This contrasts with those who have just retired, where a majority of these individuals report seeing neighbors in groups only 43 percent of the time. (See Appendix Table VI-5.)

What these findings suggest is that the schism or separation between membership in organizations in the neighborhood tends to emerge once retirement status is reached. To further explore this point, Table VI-4 presents data that address the linkage between the neighborhood and voluntary associations from a somewhat different perspective. Information is presented here in terms of whether the individual belongs exclusively to organizations where neighbors are seen, where they exclusively belong to organizations where there are no neighbors and where the individual has a mixed pattern --some groups where the neighbors are seen some where they are not.

A "mixed" pattern of neighborhood and non-neighborhood linked associational participation varies considerably by retirement status. Newly retired persons are least likely to have this pattern, while those about to retire are most likely to have such a mixed configuration. At the same time, those who have been retired for longer than a year show a mixed pattern which begins to move toward that of the persons not nearing retirement, but is still significantly lower. (See Table VI-4)

Respondents were asked whether they were aware of "someone in the neighborhood who is active in getting things done" a person "who can help with personal problems," someone "who is an officer in a local organization," or someone who "can do repairs or fix up special work for pay when you want to save money." Taking into account these four kinds of network resources, their time and status is associated with a reduction in these kinds of networks: Knowing someone in the neighborhood who is an officer is reported by 33 percent of those not nearing retirement status, and by only 20 percent of those who have been retired for a year or more. Knowing someone who is an "activist" declines from 38 percent for those nearing retirement to 24 percent for those who have been retired for more than a year. Likewise, knowing a person "who is helpful with personal problems" declines from a high of 23 percent for those nearing retirement to only 6 percent for those who have just retired. (See Table VI-5).

Collective Action on Individual Problems

It might be argued that when people are able to see a connection between their own problems and that of others, collective action is possible. There has been a great deal of discussion basically about whether seniors are indeed a group which can be politically organized. The Gray Panther movement of the 1970's is of course one expression of the large scale political participation of seniors. The famous Townsend Movement of the 1930's is of course the most significant expression of the collective political movement that can emerge from those in a retirement status.

We can examine whether the kinds of problems with which seniors and retirees deal tend to be those which are focused at the individual level and in which the kind of help they received is of this kind or those having a more collective character. For kinds of situations were discussed and questioned. The first is "People keep an eye on each other's houses when someone goes on a trip or vacation." This is the most commonly reported type of helping behavior in neighborhoods. Responses do not differ appreciably by retirement status except that those on the verge of retirement are at the highest group. 93 percent report having such help. Secondly, there is the situation of "When someone has something on their mind that is bothering them--a personal problem--people are willing to offer help." There is a high level of this reported help, again by those on the verge of retirement in contrast with other groups. If we add together both responses, we find that the group on the verge of retirement is most likely to use neighborhood helping in regard to "individual" needs of watching the house and dealing with a personal problem.

There are two situations that deal with the "collective" action of helping. The first of these is "If a local school official does a bad job, neighbors help in doing something about it." Those saying this is true in their neighborhood most often are those who have just recently retired--76 percent. Those least likely to report such help are the persons retired for a longer period of time--only 44 percent. A second situation discussed: "If a local business or industry is harming the area, people are willing to organize and protest about that problem." Here we find that it is the individuals who have just recently retired who report this is true of the neighborhood more frequently than other groups. We find that perceived neighborhood readiness for collective versus individual helping is greatest for those who have just retired. Thereafter, such perceptions decline dramatically. (See Table VI-6).

In Table VI-6 we have reconceptualized problems in terms of two types: one we might view as technical assistance with a task which Litwak would call a fairly "uniform task"--in the first case watching the house when one is gone and secondly having someone in the neighborhood who can help with home repairs. The other tasks, which we might call nonuniform, include help with a personal problem and taking action in regard to a polluting industry. Both of these might be viewed as fairly complex social behaviors--in the first instance there are a variety of ways of providing help and the second is a complex political action.

We find that for the nonuniform tasks, in six out of eight cases, a statistically significant correlation occurs with contact in the neighborhood and size and liking of the neighborhoods. This is true for only three out of eight comparisons which deal with uniform tasks. Thus, overall the measures of neighborhood liking, size, frequency of contact, and number of friends is much more significant in predicting the help or, at least, in defining the expectation of help in regard to complex social processes. In particular, the number of friends and the frequency of contact with neighbors is the most strongly correlated with both collective action on pollution problems and the solving of personal problems. It is here that we then see that social contact is itself not simply a sociability dimension, but has instrumental or utilitarian significance as well. (See Table VI-7.)

Neighbor Helping with Life Crises and Recent Concerns

The newly retired person is more likely to get help from a neighbor for "recent concerns" than is a nonretired person. By contrast, persons retired for more than one year show a sharply lower level, as do other respondents. When the measure of neighbor help is based on the percent of all problems in which a neighbor is implicated, then a different pattern emerges. Persons not approaching retirement have a 20 percent utilization pattern compared to the 38 percent for persons retired for more than a year. (See Table VI-8).

With regard to "crisis helping" (illness, a death in the family and other stressful events) we find that neighbor help is highest for those who have newly retired, with 55 percent reporting such helping. It is not significantly different for those who have been retired for a longer period of time. It appears, then, that the critical differential in neighbor help is not the one-time crisis, but in the set of recent concerns. It is here that we see, in one case, the newly retired and, in the other, the long-term retired who reports using neighborhood help to a greater degree than persons who have not entered into a retirement status.

The use of a neighbor for problem solving is, in part, a reflection that there are problems in the neighborhood to begin with. There is a strong negative correlation between liking the neighborhood and using neighborhood help for "recent concerns" (-.53). Therefore, turning to a neighbor for help is a function of the fact that the environment of the neighborhood is threatening. This reflects a significant duality in neighborhood contact: first there is the sociability function. Here people who get together for visits establish a potential basis of helping. Such contact may be the reason that they like the neighborhood. Or, turning the matter around the other way, because they like the neighborhood, they are more likely to have neighborhood friendships and contact.

Two of the nine "recent concerns" deal with neighborhood crime. People, especially those who are retired, may be turning to their neighbors because of crime fears. We have already seen these are higher for this group, although the actual experience of being a victim of crime is not significantly higher than for other respondents.) To what extent is it true then that neighbor help is a function of the negative aspects of the environment and is in turn translated into using the neighbor for help with crime problems of the neighborhood? Forty-five percent of those persons retired for more than a year use neighbor help for neighborhood problems. For those who have just recently retired or who are not nearing retirement status, the percentages are higher--54 and 58 percent respectively. At the same time there is a much higher use of the neighbor for other concerns. Thirty-three percent of those who retired a year or more before the first interview report neighbor help for non-neighborhood concerns. This contrasts with only 17 percent for those who have just retired, and 14 percent for those not nearing retirement status. The ratio of helping for neighborhood problems to non-neighborhood problems is smaller for those who have been retired for a significant period of time. These findings suggest the functional substitution role that neighbor help plays for those who have been retired for longer than one year. (See Table VI-9)

What about the type of help offered by the neighbor? Does that differ by retirement status? Here we see the five basic kinds of helping behaviors that we have utilized in the survey. "Listening" behavior is most likely to be given by a neighbor where the person is on the verge of retirement. The "asking questions" and "listening" are the behaviors that neighbors tend to be associated with for this group rather than, "referral" help. By contrast, those that have recently retired are least likely to receive "asking questions" help and most likely to receive "referral." There is a tendency for "referral" help by a neighbor to increase as one enters upon retirement status. This result suggests the linkage role that the neighborhood can play. (See Table VI-10).

Summary

In this chapter we have reviewed a number of indicators of how people see help in their neighborhood, what kinds of problems they use neighbors to help with and what correlation exists between the seeking of help from neighbors and the perception of the quality of neighboring and neighborhood. For those who are seniors (age sixty-five or older) helping for "recent concerns" and "life crises" is not correlated with the frequency of visiting with neighbors or the number of neighborhood friends. Such correlations do tend to exist for persons below that age, although these relationships are very weak.

We find that the newly retired tend to be heavily specialized in neighborhood-linked organizations and to be less likely to belong to exclusively non-neighborhood-based voluntary associations. The findings of Table VI-4 suggested that if an individual belongs to a mixed pattern of groups (where neighbors are seen and not seen) there is a kind of social integration or networking that can occur. That is to say, information, ideas and experiences in organizations not neighborhood linked are combined with organizational experiences which are neighborhood focuses. Thus, the two, by co-mingling, can be a basis of the flow of ideas and information, innovation and a sense of linkage which may be a significant way to define the integration of the individual in society as a whole. What appears to occur is that individuals who newly enter upon retirement status are least likely to have this kind of linkage through their diverse patterns of organizational participation. Those who are retired for a longer time tend to restore some of that linkage, but it does not really attain the level of individuals who are younger and not retired.

As we shall describe in subsequent analyses, neighboring can provide a "network" capacity for seniors and retirees. This is a critical dimension of their social situation and one of the functions that the neighborhood can play is to create the possibility of ties to other social arenas. The increase in "referral" helping by neighbors for those who retire clearly supports this functional argument.

CHART VI-2

Perceived Size of Neighborhood and Interviewers' Evaluation of
Public Facilities in Relation to Risk Score for Persons 65 or older
(Percent Above the Median Score)

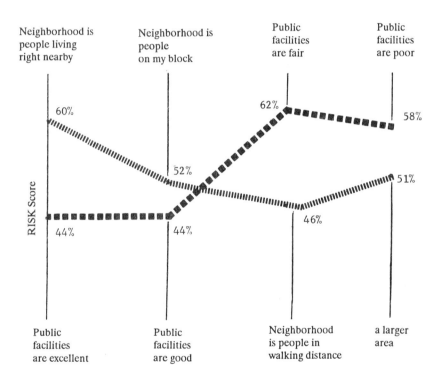

CHART VI-3

Frequency of Visiting with Neighbors in Relation
to RISK Score for Persons 65 or older

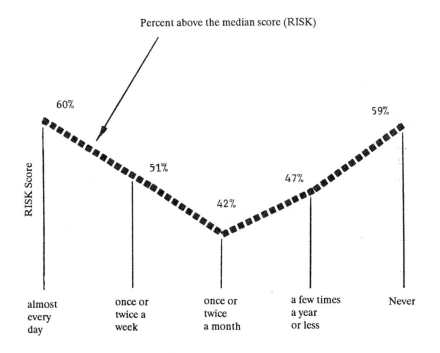

Percent above the median score (RISK)

60%

59%

51%

47%

42%

RISK Score

almost
every
day

once or
twice a
week

once or
twice
a month

a few times
a year
or less

Never

TABLE VI-1

Perceived Size of Neighborhood
"When you think of the area you consider
your neighborhood, what comes to mind?"

	Retired more than 1 year before interview	Retired within the last year	To retire within 1 year after interview	Other persons inter-viewed
People living right nearby (across the street or next door)	22%	42%+	13%−	21%
People on my block	38	38	37	32
People within walking distance	24	15−	29	24
A larger area	15−	6−	21+	23+
TOTAL	99%	101%	100%	100%

TABLE VI-2

**Frequency of Visiting Neighbors and Amount of Close
Friendships in the Neighborhood**

	Retired more than 1 year before interview	Retired within the last year	To retire within 1 year after interview	Other persons inter- viewed
Frequency of Visiting				
Almost every day	5%	4%	5%	5%
Once or twice a week	12	15	13	14
Once or twice a month	13	22+	10	15
A few times a year or less	33	33	35	36
Never	36+	26	38+	29
TOTAL	99%	100%	101%	99%

Number of Close Friends in the Neighborhood				
10 or more	14%	6%	25%+	11%
6 to 9	14	6	5	13
3 to 5	23	31+	23	22
1 or 2	25	44+	23	29
None	23	13-	25	25
TOTAL	99%	100%	101%	100%

TABLE VI-3

Number of Organizations Respondent Belongs to Where Neighbors are Seen

	Retired more than 1 year before interview	Retired within the last year	To retire within 1 year after interview	Other persons inter- viewed
None	45%	38%	28%	39%
One	27	30	28	21
Two or more	28−	32	44+	40+
TOTAL	100%	100%	100%	100%
Belong to a block club or neighborhood association	16%	23%+	13%	16%

TABLE VI-4

**Mixed or Uniform Membership in Organizations:
Neighbors Seen or Not Seen**

	Retired more than 1 year before interview	Retired within the last year	To retire within 1 year after interview	Other persons interviewed
See neighbors in all organizations R belongs to	28%	47%+	20%	23%
Mixed pattern– see neighbors at some groups, not at others	44–	30–	55+	51+
Do not see neighbors in organizations R belongs to	19	13–	20	20
Don't belong to organizations	9	9	5	6
TOTAL	100%	99%	100%	100%

TABLE VI-5

Linkages to Reputational Helpers and Organizational Leaders

	Retired more than 1 year before interview	Retired within the last year	To retire within 1 year after interview	Other persons inter- viewed
Know local people who do home or car repairs	19%	13% −	23%	27%
Know someone in the local area who is an officer or very active in an organization	20% −	27%	28%	33%
Know a local person who is "active if you want to get something done"	24%	28%	38% +	36% +
Know a local person to help with personal problems	14% −	6% −	23% +	19%

TABLE VI-6

**Neighborhood Individual or Collection
Action Helping**

	Retired more than 1 year before interview	Retired within the last year	To retire within 1 year after interview	Other persons inter- viewed
	Percent "true"			
People keep an eye on each others' houses	89%	83%	93%	87%
People will be willing to help with a personal problem	58%	61%	69%+	56%
Total	147%	144%	162%	143%
If a local school official does a bad job, neighbors help in doing something about it	44%	76%+	56%	52%
If a local business or industry is harming the area, people are willing to organize and protest about the problem	62%	87%+	64%	63%
Total	106%	163%	120%	115%
Grand Total	253%	307%	282%	258%

TABLE VI-7

Correlation between Contact with Neighbors, Perception of Neighborhood and Neighbor Individual and Collective Action Helping

	Watch house	Do home and car repairs	Take school action	Take action on business
Like the neighborhood	+.28*	+.06	+.29*	+.23*
Perceived size of neighborhood	−.03	−.09	+.04	+.04
Frequency of visits with neighbors	+.24*	+.14	+.34*	+.56*
Number of close friends in the neighborhood	+.29	+.19	+.68*	+.41*

*

Gamma values significant at .05 level.

TABLE VI-8

**Extent of Neighbor Helping for Recent Concerns
and Life Crises**

	Retired more than 1 year before interview	Retired within the last year	To retire within 1 year after interview	Other persons inter-viewed
Percent of persons with one or more recent concerns using neighbor helping	28%	41%	25%	27%
Percent of all recent concerns where neighbor is used as a neighbor	38%	31%	33%	20%
Diffusion*	+10%	−10%	+8%	−7%
Neighbor help for life crisis	51%	55%	44%	48%

*

Extent to which percent of persons using a given helper matches frequency of helper use for recent concerns. A "+" denotes neighbor is being used for more than one problem per user.

TABLE VI-9

Degree to Which Neighbor Help is Limited
to Neighborhood
Problems

	Neighborhood problems	Other problems	Ratio
	"A"	"B"	
Retired more than 1 year before interview	45%	33%	1.4:1
	(n=47)	(n=52)	
Retired within the last year	58%	17%	3.4:1
	(n=12)	(n=23)	
To retire within 1 year after interview	54%	25%	2.2:1
	(n=13)	(n=32)	
Other persons interviewed	54%	14%	3.9:1
	(n=446)	(n=2472)	

TABLE VI-10

Type of Help Provided by Neighbor for Recent Concerns

	Retired more than 1 year before interview	Retired within the last year	To retire within 1 year after interview	Other persons inter-viewed
Listening	86%	80%	100%+	79%
Asking questions	45%	30%−	57%+	54%+
Showing a new way to look at the problem	15%	10%	14%	14%
Referral	27%+	20%+	0%−	8%−
Taking action	7%	0%	14%	11%

CHAPTER VII

NEIGHBORHOOD SOCIAL FABRIC AND THE HELPING
NETWORKS OF THE AGING AND RETIRED

A key focus of the analysis of helping is the role of different social structures of the localities in which individuals reside. This focus directs attention to the "context" within which given problems are developed and what kinds of resources are used or perceived as valuable. As we shall subsequently discover, neighborhood is not simply an objective physical setting, but involves a set of actual and potential social anchoring points in terms of pathways to helping.

Based on a series of earlier studies[6], three dimensions are employed to define significant neighborhood variations that are important to help seeking and problem coping: 1) the extent of individual identification with the area; 2) the degree of social exchanges within the neighborhood; and 3) the extent to which the area is explicitly linked to the larger community. Additional work with this classification scheme has led to modifications and the effort to treat the typology as sufficient to cover divergent social class, ethnic identification, and location within the metropolitan area (see Chart VII-1). Using measures of neighbor contacts, associational patterns, and local area ties, the 28 areas sampled in the study were originally divided into the six types of areas given below:

The Integral Neighborhood--A locale with 1) high levels of formal and informal interaction with one another; 2) manifest high levels of contact with local government; 3) high levels of reported voting in the last national election; 4) strong commitments to remaining in the neighborhood; and 5) strong positive attitudes toward the area. Here are quotations from the thumbnail sketches of interviewers with seniors and retirees living in such locales:

> Well, I think it's a good neighborhood and a well-kept neighborhood. It's more like a small town in itself. We have our churches, schools, and shopping center.

> I can't think of a thing (that would cause me to want to move). I've had twenty-six happy years here.

> R. and wife talked about being old, that all their friends were dying or already dead, and that young people didn't want to bother with them. They have a very large garden and often mentioned it. It seems very important to their lives and in how they relate to their neighbors. They often give food and flowers away and seem to talk to neighbors often. R. mentioned that they don't do many repairs, but that the neighbors help them with anything major.

> Oh there are a lot of things good about it (the neighborhood): The Rosedale Park Association, more neighborly living, people have respect for their neighbors.

> As of now I can't think of anything (that would cause me to want to move) except the rising tax rate.

The Parochial Neighborhood--A locale with 1) extensive formal and informal interaction with one another; 2) positive attitudes towards the neighborhood; and 3) low levels of social and political participation outside of the local area. Here is one description of this type of setting:

> There is a ball park across the street from this home. R. didn't think anyplace she lived would be any different. She didn't seem to know about her neighbors or want to be neighborly. She believed in reading the newspapers and she believed in what they said. When asked what she liked best about living in her neighborhood, she responded, 'No place would be any different from here. It's alright. Why should I move?' Across the street there are ball games and groups of teenagers gather there. They get kind of loud, but she has told them and they're good about it.

While the self-contained character of the parochial neighborhood is a positive asset, this very fact may become a liability for some retirees and seniors:

> This lady basically lives alone. She has a son who is considered disabled and doesn't know where he goes. He's been divorced and has some kind of problem. She is a retiree who is on a fixed income and she constantly referred to the increase in utility bills and taxes and how hard it is to manage the home.

> She has only a son who lives next door and a daughter to do her shopping or take her to the doctor and so doesn't get out very much.

The Stepping-stone Neighborhood--A locale with 1) extensive formal and informal contact; 2) no pronounced positive reference group orientation in the local area; and 3) extensive participation in the political process of the larger community. Stepping-stone locals reflect the rapid changes that may occur in neighborhoods and the negative consequences that may result:

> R. seems very upset about the situation in the neighborhood. 'People just went crazy. I just don't know what to say.' The reason that she's living there is because of a niece. She said that her niece went to the market down the street and couldn't get to the market for the young fellows pulling on her. Her niece is 'nothing but 10 years old.' She managed to get away from them and came running home. 'She came for me, but I couldn't help her cause I'm a old lady. What could I do? My neighbors had called.'

A major reason for seniors being isolated in Stepping-stone settings is the sharp age split and social distance that exists there:

> R. retired some time ago. His wife goes to work to help ends meet. Her cousin stays there while she works. 'With everything going up so high, the people on assistance are better off than we are. Most of the people in the neighborhood are young and they notice you and look at you suspiciously as if to say: What are you doing in this neighborhood? I just smile and keep going. I didn't have trouble getting their account number.' They said, 'Be careful.'

The Transitory Neighborhood--A locale with 1) low positive identification with the local area; 2) little formal or informal interaction; and 3) participation in the larger community to a moderate or high degree. Here is one respondents comments:

> When asked what things about this neighborhood R. liked best, she replied, 'Nothing anymore. It used to be all nice people, but now people who are moving in have changed.'

Physical deterioration is a common by-product of the transitory area:

> When asked what things about this neighborhood could cause R. to want to move: 'People don't keep places up. They throw bottles, trash, cans on your lawn. People parked in front in cars. Don't know who they are. Dogs run loose.'

> Their home was broken into in August, 1974, during morning hours (8:00-12:00 a.m.) while they were on vacation. All the appliances were stolen, taken in a truck. The neighbors were unable to identify anything. The family here does not appear to be too neighborly. The police were no help--even though all serial numbers were recorded. R was quite disgusted with neighbors and police.

> R. is the type of person who does not neighbor or mix well with outsiders. She has just been home from the hospital three weeks. When I came her husband and grown son were home which helped the situation in obtaining an interview right then. She is sorry now they moved here--her children are grown, but will tolerate the kids. The children playing basketball bother her most. She bought a big German Shepard dog to keep outsiders away. The neighborhood is made up of mainly young people with young children.

The Anomic Neighborhood--A locale which 1) lacks formal and informal ties to the local area; 2) does not have a high level of participation in the larger community; and 3) lacks strong positive identification to the neighborhood. Here is a description of one such setting:

> Respondent's apartment is part of Cherryhill Manor Apartments.... Respondent had a hip injury last year forcing him to a medical retirement. He sold his grocery store and home....to move into these apartments. He hasn't had a chance to meet neighbors. The apartment complex consists mainly of retirees and young working couples; no children or pets are allowed.

Often the anomic setting is one that seniors feel trapped in:

Respondent is widowed and 'disabled' by high blood pressure. She says she would work if possible. She keeps her grandson for company. (His mother is on A.D.C.) Robbery in the neighborhood disturbs her, but she has a very low income and says, 'Where could I move?'

Helping Networks of Seniors Based on Neighborhood Contexts

Let us now evaluate how helping for persons 65 or older is affected by various neighborhood contexts. We begin by comparing the differences in *kinds of helpers* used. In Table VII-1, a "+" and "-" denotes an above or below average amount of use of one kind of helper for recent concerns. We find that that in transitory or anomic settings, help from the spouse tends to be higher than average and is below average in the steppingstone setting. Relative help is also high in the anomic and steppingstone context, but low in a transitory neighborhood. The integral neighborhood is characterized by less than average spouse helping and less than average use of formal helpers.

The parochial setting tends to have more than average formal helping, and this is also true of the diffuse setting. By contrast, the steppingstone local has higher than average neighbor, friend and relative helping. The transitory setting and the anomic both tend to have higher than average co-worker helping. (See Table VII-1.)

In terms of the type of help provided we find that the integral setting is characterized by more than average "referral" and "action" helping and less than average "showing a-new-way" helping. By contrast, in the parochial setting focuses on help that involves asking questions rather than referral. The diffuse setting characterized by a combination of above average referral, action helping and in showing a person a new way to look at a problem. There is below average listening and asking questions. The steppingstone setting tends to be higher than average in all forms of helping except that of asking questions. The transitory setting tends to be above average in listening and average in other types of behavior. The anomic setting is below average in both action and referral helping and above average in listening behavior and showing a person a new way to look at a problem. (See Appendix Table VII-1.)

On an overall basis Table VII-2 suggests a set of differential emphases in types of help provided the different neighborhood contexts. Moreover, the pattern we find for seniors is not the same in many instances as for the general population. (See *Warren*, 1981.) In the case of seniors and other persons as well, the integral neighborhood type emerges as the one emphasizing referral and action helping. However, in the case of seniors, we find similar helping emphases are also found in diffuse and steppingstone contexts. Both seniors and others surveyed receive less referral or action helping in the anomic neighborhood setting than in other residential contexts. For seniors the Parochial setting is also restrictive in this regard.

The findings noted provide clues for the hypothesis that the self-contained world of parochial neighborhood may be far less supportive than it is isolating for seniors. At the same time, the somewhat turbulent pattern of the steppingstone neighborhood offers the virtue of linkages to the outside world. Seniors may benefit from the helping roles of younger families who may be only short-term residents but who may bring valuable contacts and helping resources that the more stable but insulated parochial setting cannot provide. (See TABLE VII-2)

There is virtually no difference between neighborhood types in terms of the probability of having someone nearby to watch over the house. Yet, in terms of help with a personal problem, fairly large differences emerge. The diffuse setting is highest in perceiving this kind of help while the transitory setting is lowest. With regard to knowing someone who can do home repairs there is also a clear difference between neighborhoods. The parochial and the diffuse settings are both significantly higher than other locales in having this kind of help available. The integral and anomic neighborhoods differ sharply. The steppingstone neighborhood is least likely to have this kind of resource available. (See Appendix Table VII-2.)

The stepping stone neighborhood is generally higher in regard to helping with a problem of the school principal and of a polluting business. The parochial neighborhood also shows a high degree of perceived resources such for "collective action." By contrast, both the transitory and the anomic settings are low. The diffuse setting is inconsistent: below average in terms of the perceived availability of help on school action, yet above in regard to expected action on a polluting industry. (See TABLE VII-3)

Does the neighborhood type itself produce a significant difference in the well-being of seniors in each of these settings? Let us first examine the percentage of persons above the median RISK score by neighborhood. We find that the integral setting is the most "buffering" of stress in the sense that only 32 percent of seniors living in such locales are above the mean on the RISK score. However, we find that the parochial setting does not emerge as conducive to well-being: 62 percent of seniors are above the median RISK score. The stepping stone and parochial settings are both associated with the highest risk to well-being. This had been suggested in several of the thumbnail descriptions of respondent interviews.

While it is clear that there is a relationship between well-being of seniors and neighborhood type, the cause is not self-evident. It could be speculated, for example, that in the steppingstone neighborhood the senior is a minority person in the sense that they are not on the path of upward social mobility characteristic of such neighborhoods, and are therefore likely to be excluded from a number of aspects of neighborhood life. At the same time, the parochial setting, which emphasizes privacy, may be precisely what seniors do not need in the sense of integration into the larger society.

The fact that the integral setting is one which has a combination of strong internal structure as well as linkage to the outside may well explain why this is the setting which is most associated with well-beingof seniors and retirees. It is also this linkage to the outside that may explain why the transitory neighborhood is less of a threat to well-being than one might predict, based on the general typology. (See TABLE VII-4)

Perceived Neighborhood Fabric

In the general study it was found that a very powerful predictor of individual well-being was the extent to which the individual thought the neighborhood had a particular social form or not. Let us now explore the subjective definition of neighborhood fabric as it applies to seniors and retirees. A series of four different components of the subjects' assessment of neighborhood includes first, that indicated by the question "Do people in this neighborhood have many things in common? Some things in common? Or a few things in common?" Responses to this question indicate that a smaller proportion of retirees, (both newly retired and those retired for more than a year), compared to other respondents indicate that their neighborhood is characterized by people having "some" or "many" things in common.

The second of perceived neighborhood the component is indicated by the question, "Are there people who in this neighborhood get together many times, a few times or hardly ever during the year?" We find that the persons who have been retired for more than a year are at least likely to say that their neighborhood is characterized by people getting together "a few" or "many" times. By constrast, this is perceived to be true most for those who are newly retired.

The third indicator of subject neighborhood fabric has to do with linkages to outside groups, the particular question being: "Do many, a few, or hardly any people in this neighborhood keep active in groups outside of the local area?" Here, we find that it is persons retired for more than a year who see the least external linkages: 49 percent versus 65 percent of the newly retired; and 69 percent for those who are not near retirement.

A fourth indicator of neighborhood social fabric is the extent to which people see turnover occuring in their residential area. The specfic question is, "Are there many people who move in and out of this neighborhood, a few or hardly any?" Those on the verge of retirement are most likely to report neighborhood turnover as low while those who have recently retired show a sharply different perspective. (See TABLE VII-5)

The respondents retired for more than one year tend to have a less common sense of neighborhood turnover.

Those who have been retired for more than a year see their neighborhood as weak in three out of four aspects of social fabric. Those who are newly retired tend to see the neighborhood as having a high degree of social contact, an average degree of linkages to the outside, but below average commitment in terms of things held in common. Thus, we might say that the long-term retired person perceives their neighborhood as anomic while the newly retired sees it as stepping stone. The person on the verge of retirement and persons sees neighborhood as strong in two dimensions--linkages to the outside and things held in common by other--those in the same residential setting.

When we examine the relationship between the various indicators of perceived neighborhood social fabric and problem helping, some important results emerge. Fourteen of sixteen correlations are significant for problems with school or industries, someone to help with repairs, and finding help in watching one's home. The strongest correlations are found for the two "collective action" situations.

The variable of liking the neighborhood is related to taking action on an industry that is polluting (gamma = +.29). Even stronger as correlate is the perceptions about neighbors getting together or the extent to which neighbors perceived people being active outside groups; the correlations respectively being +.67 and +.52. (See Table VII-6)

While, in general, all of the elements are additive in their effects on helping, that of having neighbors watch one's house shows a significant negative correlation (-.40) with people being active in outside groups. Here, seniors seem to be suggesting that if everyone is socially active outside of the neighborhood, they may not be available to help in watching one's home. In terms of knowing someone to do repairs, we find that there are some clear differences based on the degree of perceived fabric of the neighborhood. Those seeing a lot of people in the neighborhood active in outside groups are also those who tend to know about someone who can help with repairs in the neighborhood.

When seniors find that they have many things in common with their neighbors, 96 percent of the time they say that neighbors are willing to watch over the house. If they do not know whether neighbors have many things in common, this kind of help drops to 62 percent. Where neighbors are seen as getting together socially, 98 percent of the time seniors say that there is someone to watch their home. This contrasts with 71 percent of the time where they report not knowing whether their neighbors get together or not.

In terms of personal problems, having a sense that neighbors share things in common shows a gamma of +.63, perceived getting together of neighbors, +.65 and neighbors active in outside groups, +.47. In terms of things in common in the neighborhood, there is a modest relationship, +.17, while perceived getting together is +.26, and neighbors active in groups is +.32.

Several indicators of perceived neighborhood social fabric correlate with the RISK score Seeing neighbors having "manay" or "some" things in common, getting together "many" or "a few" times is associated with the lowest RISK scores.

The measure of perceived involvement of neighbors in non-neighborhood groups is curvilinear in its relation to the RISK score; low where either many neighbors are seen as active or few. This means that a situation of perceiving many things in common with neighbors *and* seeing them as visiting frequently but seeing few as active in external groups minimizes the RISK score. Thus, both a "+ + +" and a "+ +-" pattern (refer back to Chart VII-1) is equivalent to a perceived "parochial" or "integral" neighborhood. When seniors report consistently on all three social fabric measures that they "don't know" this is associated with the highest RISK score. This may be viewed as a functional equivalent of a perceived "Anomic" neighborhood content. (See CHART VII-2)

Summary

In this chapter we have reviewed a number of the indicators of objective and subjective neighborhood types which have been employed in the core study as well as in previous research by the author.[5] This typology has yielded results which suggest that there are important differences in neighborhood social fabric characteristics linked to the kinds of resources that seniors and retirees have available. For example, those in the objectively defined integral, diffuse and steppingstone settings are more likely to get "action" and "referral" helping than in parochial, transitory or anomic settings. In neighborhoods where there is a weak commitment to the neighborhood, (low interaction and low linkages to the outside) there is a high degree of more passive helping such as listening and showing a new way to look at a problem, but less referral or action help.

We find that both objective and subjective neighborhood types are very powerful predictors of the possibility of collective action on the part of the neighborhood as it is experienced by seniors. In turn, the particular role of subjectively defined neighborhood social fabric seems to be a greater one than that of objective indicators. These are similar results to the overall core study findings for non-seniors.

There is evidence that in the objectively defined steppingstone neighborhood--which tends to give a variety of help generally to its members--that seniors may indeed often be isolated from these resources. The fact that the anomic neighborhood may be objectively weak apparently does not prevent the existence of a wide range of immediate neighbor helping. While this neighborhood type is "objectively" weak, "perceptually" speaking it may be stronger and may have significant resources. In addition, the parochial setting (in the objective sense, one in which there is a clear boundary and insulation from the outside) may indeed be a neighborhood which is seen by seniors as an unduly isolating environment.

Our findings underscore the fact that we may look at neighborhoods in terms of two levels of reference. One is the one-to-one neighboring that may be associated with help and which may be the basis of an individual identifying with a small scale unit of neighborhood. At the same time, it is clear that the well-being of seniors is more likely to be protected where the neighborhood is defined as a larger unit than immediate neighbors or even the block as a whole but extends to the walking distance definition of neighborhood.

We can recognize that in the two levels of neighborhood analysis, there are a couple of possibilities: 1) that individuals may perceive themselves to be in a strong neighborhood and will therefore make use of those resources; or 2) they may perceive themselves to be in a weak neighborhood and not find or make use of resources. A serious discrepancy may exist, however, between the perception and the reality. A person may underestimate what is actually available and will be isolated from the potential help of a strong but perceptual or weak neighborhood. Thus local resources will be used so exclusively that other outside resources will be unnecessarily ignored. To the extent that seniors perceive their neighborhood to have active contact between neighbors, then this will increase the likelihood that they will use such resources. Thus, there is evidence that the objectively defined parochial neighborhood may not really be a subjectively defined parochial neighborhood, and therefore there may be an underutilization of its resources to a significant degree. Thus, the transitory neighborhood may, because it has linkages to the outside, be perceived by seniors who happen to belong to the core of oldtimers in that locale to have a more effective neighborhood than many of the newcomers do. This is precisely the opposite of the situation in the steppingstone neighborhood where the seniors find themselves to be the leftovers and the new corners are part of a social mobility pattern which then links them to many networks that they, as seniors, are exclided from.

CHART VII-1

**A Typology of Neighborhoods Based on Social Organization and
Reference Group Orientation**

Neighborhood as a Reference Group	Type	Formal and Informal Organization	Orientation to Larger Community
Neighborhood is a Positive Reference Group	Integral	+	+
	Parochial	+	−
	Diffuse	−	−
Neighborhood is not a Positive Reference Group	Stepping-stone	+	+
	Transitory	−	+
	Anomic	−	−

TABLE VII-1

**Neighborhood Type and the Type of Helper
Used for Recent Concerns**

	Spouse	Relative	Friend	Neighbor	Co-worker	Formal helper
Integral	−					−
Parochial						+
Diffuse						+
Stepping stone	−	+	+	+		
Transitory	+	−	−	+	+	
Anomic	+	+			+	

TABLE VII-2

Type of Helping Behavior Provided
in Relation to Neighborhood Type

	Listening	Asking questions	Showing a new way	Referring	Taking action
Integral	−		−	+	+
Parochial	−	+	−	−	−
Diffuse	−	−	+	+	+
Stepping stone	+		+	+	+
Transitory					
Anomic	+		+	−	−

TABLE VII-3

Neighborhood Type and Collective Action Helping

	Neighbors will do something if school official is doing a bad job area	Neighbors will organize and protest about a business that is harming the
Integral	58%	71%+
Parochial	74%+	68%
Diffuse	43%−	78%+
Steppingstone	74%+	79%+
Transitory	28%−	47%−
Anomic	36%−	52%−

TABLE VII-4

**Neighborhood Type in Relation to RISK Score
for Persons Age 65 or Older**

	Mean score	Percent above median
Integral	10.9	32%
Parochial	14.1	62%
Diffuse	12.8	51%
Steppingstone	14.3	60%
Transitory	11.9	42%
Anomic	11.7	46%

TABLE VII-5

Perceived Social Fabric of the Neighborhood

	Retired more than 1 year before interview	Retired within the last year	To retire within 1 year after interview	Other persons interviewed
See people in the area having many or some things in common	56%	58%	68%+	66%+
See neighbors getting together many or a few times for visits	39%−	56%+	43%	47%
See many or a few neighbors who keep active in outside groups	49%−	65%+	62%+	69%+
See many or a few people moving in and out of the neighborhood	45%−	57%+	35%−	62%+

TABLE VII-6

**Correlation Between Perceived Neighborhood
Social Fabric and Perceived Problem
Help and Action
(persons age 65 or older)**

	Watch the house	Know someone to do home or car repairs	People will do something about bad school official	People will take action on business harming the area
Perceived things in common	+.27*	+.17	+.21*	+.64*
Perceived in getting together of neighbors	−.07	+.26*	+.67*	+.65*
Perceived activity of neighbors in non-neighborhood groups	−.40*	+.32*	+.52*	+.47*
Perceived neighbors moving in and out (turnover)	−.22*	−.30*	−.38*	−.30*

*
Gamma coefficients significant at .05 level or beyond.

CHART VII-2
Perceived Neighborhood Social Fabric in Relation
to RISK Score for Persons age 65 or older

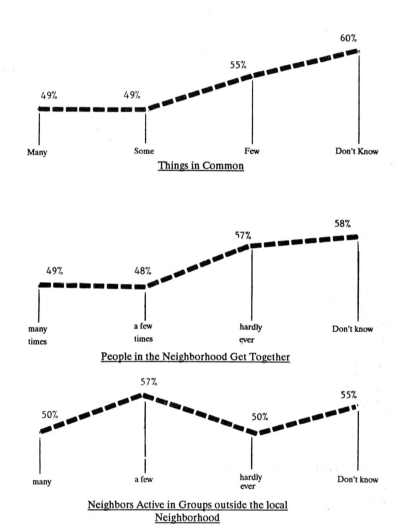

RISK Score

| 49% | 49% | 55% | 60% |
| Many | Some | Few | Don't Know |

Things in Common

| 49% | 48% | 57% | 58% |
| many times | a few times | hardly ever | Don't know |

People in the Neighborhood Get Together

| 50% | 57% | 50% | 55% |
| many | a few | hardly ever | Don't know |

Neighbors Active in Groups outside the local
Neighborhood

CHAPTER VIII

SOME EVIDENCE OF THE COMMUNITY EFFECT ON THE HELPING NETWORKS OF THE AGING

As was noted in Chapter II the sample design of the study included a cross-section, random sampling of eight communities surrounding the city of Detroit. While each of these locales had separate neighborhoods that were surveyed, in the present chapter we treat social patterns that derive from the particular municipality as a whole. Figure 1 shows the location of the selected cities in relation to Detroit.

An Index of the Strength of Community Helping Systems

The analysis of community helps us to develop a basic view of how one community may differ from another in terms of the helping roles found within each locale. Our strategy involves selecting measures of the volume and content of helping as the way to define relatively more or less "healthy" communities in regard to helping capacity. In effect, the question we explore at this point is: "Given a 'recent concern' how well is it coped with in community 'A' versus community 'B'?"

We employed a total of four measures to construct our "barometer" of community helping "health." First, we compared the number of helpers per problem found in each locale. This is the "extensivity" index used in earlier chapters. There are rather sharp community differences here. The highest community--Royal Oak--has twice the number of different kinds of helpers per problem on the average as the lowest community--Mt. Clemens. (See FIGURE 1)

The second comparison is that of total numbers of the same or different helpers for each recent concern experienced. Here, a similar doubling from highest to lowest occurs. A third community comparison in regard to helping is that of "intensivity"--the average number of different kinds of helping behaviors that occur for recent concerns. On this measure the eight municipalities do not differ in any marked degree. The highest level is found for Lincoln Park--1.8 per problem versus the low of 1.3 for Pontiac.

The fourth indicator of community "health" is the probability of having a "recent concern" without the use of any helpers whatsoever. This "isolation" measure shows some important variation for the eight municipalities sampled. The high is 19 percent in Warren, Michigan; the low 10 percent in both Royal Oak and St. Clair Shores.

What happens if we put the four indicators together to form a community helping scale--a way to define the strength of helping systems in one locale versus another? In fact, communities show a fairly consistent pattern from one index to the next. When added, a clustering of three groups occurs with rather large intervals between. At the "high" end of the barometer is Royal Oak closely followed by Lincoln Park and St. Clair Shores. These three are similar to one another but when ranked are a significant distance away from the next community on the scale. (See TABLE VIII-1)

The "Healthiest" Communities

Scoring at the top of the health or helping strength index Royal Oak is a rather densely settled older suburb of Detroit. In spite of its being a middle to upper-middle class community, its median family income is $13,600 per year. Royal Oak has a more "urban" feel than many of the other newer suburbs.

Just nine miles southwest and downriver from downtown Detroit, Lincoln Park is the second smallest community in the sample with a population of 53,000 packed into slightly less than six square miles. Although not incorporated as a city until 1925, Lincoln Park was one of the earliest of the French settlements outside of Fort Detroit. It remained a small, largely rural community until Henry Ford's offer of $5 per day for working in the auto plants brought in workers looking for a pleasant residential area near the factories (Lincoln Park is less than three miles from the huge Ford River Rouge complex). The next spurt of growth came in the 1940's with the war production mobilization and the post-war upswing in the auto industry. Although Lincoln Park is heavily blue collar, it is a relatively prosperous community with a median family income in 1970 of slightly over $12,000 a year.

Completing the triumvirate of "healthiest" communities is St. Clair Shores. This small (nearly the same size as Royal Oak), lakeside suburb is dominated by comfortable homes and a dense development of marinas and lakeside recreation areas. Incorporated in 1951, St. Clair Shores had explosive growth during the 1950's when its population increased 287 percent to 76,000. This was followed, however, by a rapid deceleration of growth-- only a 15 percent increase in the sixties--as the relatively small land area was quickly developed to capacity. In 1970 the population stood at 88,000, larger than Pontiac but on a little more than half the land area. The city is predominantly residential in character--there are only 73 industrial establishments with 1 out of 5 of these employ more than 20 people.

While a majority--53 percent of the work force--are in white-collar occupations, fewer of these are in the professional and technical areas than any other of the white-collar communities in the sample. Much of the city's early growth was based on the upward mobility of blue-collar, skilled workers. The median family income of $13,598 a year places it in the middle range of the communities in the study.

Two Medium-Strength Communities

Clearly differentiated on the four helping system measures from the top cluster are two communities that are grouped as "medium healthy." Both are among the most affluent in the sample of municipalities. Ranked fourth among the eight locales, Livonia is the shape of a perfect square being constituted by a single Northwest ordinance 36 square mile township. This sprawling suburb lies west of Detroit. Incorporated as a city in 1950, it is a product of the post-World War II suburbanization of cities. Between 1950 and 1960 its population increased 280 percent, from just over 17,000 to almost 67,000. In the decade of the sixties it increased another 65 percent to 110,000. The city is composed predominantly of large, relatively expensive housing developments. In style it is very much a middle-to upper-class, white-collar suburb.

The median annual family income of Livonia in 1970 was over $15,000, making it the wealthiest of the eight sample communities. It is also one of the highest in formal education as well, with 15 percent of the adults having completed four years of college. This level of education and income is reflected in the occupational structure with 60 percent of the work force in white-collar jobs. It also has the fewest people (of the sample communities) below the poverty line: only 2 percent of the city's families.

If Royal Oak is an example of the older, stable and somewhat modest yet dignified white-collar suburb, Troy is just the opposite. It is one of the youngest and fastest growing suburbs in Detroit with a reputation for fast economic expansion and a just as fast lifestyle for the many singles and young marrieds that have dominated its recent growth. Incorporated in 1955 Troy has more than doubled its population between 1960 and 1970, from 19,402 to 39,412. In 1972 the population stood at 46,800, an increase of almost 19 percent in just two years. Troy is a large, formerly rural farming area, covering 33 square miles. Located about a 30 to 40 minute drive from downtown Detroit, it, in many ways, embodies the abandonment by business of the central city for the promise of rich suburban markets, fewer social problems and comparatively little crime. New office buildings dot the major arteries of the city.

Low-Helping-Strength Communities

Below the middle cluster of communities, three cities form a group widely separated in the helping index values from those we have just described. These three municipalities are largely blue collar, but have a number of characteristics that make each unlike the other in several important ways. The first of these "least" healthy communities ranks sixth on the average of the four indicators--this is Pontiac, Michigan. The city is solidly blue collar with 65 percent of the work force in manual occupations. Named after a rebellious Indian chieftain, this city has a unique mixture of inner city slums (where the black population tends to be clustered) and a rural periphery intertwined with lakes and recreational facilities. Its major industry is a large General Motors automobile assembly plant (its namesake is one of the five GM offerings) and truck-bus manufacturing facility.

The median annual family income in Pontiac in 1970 was $9,681, the lowest in the sample. Only 5 percent of the adults have completed four or more years of college. It also has the least stable family life of any of the sample communities with nearly 10 percent of the adults either separated or divorced, by far the highest in the communities studied. Pontiac is one of the two communities in the study with more than a barely discernable non-white population; over one-quarter of the city's population is non-white.

The growth of Pontiac in recent years has almost come to a halt. Its days of glory and greatest growth came in the early part of this century with the birth and early development of the auto industry. Between 1910 and 1920 the population increased 135 percent. In the twenties it jumped another 90 percent, but with the depression growth came almost to a halt followed by modest or very low growth since then. In 1970 the population was 85,279.

Closely following Pontiac and ranked next to the lowest of eight communities is Warren, Michigan. Another large suburb (36 square miles) it was the fourth largest city in Michigan in 1970. Built in part by the flight of auto workers from Detroit's industrial plants and the plants themselves from the perceived racial and crime problems of Detroit, the need for large tracts of land by manufacturing plants spurred growth here.

For six straight years in the late fifties Warren was the fastest growing city in the United States. It doubled and even quadrupled its population every year in this period. In the fifties its population jumped 1,000 percent from a village of 727 to a city of 89,246. In the sixties Warren's population slowed but still managed a 100 percent increase to 180,000. Industrial expansion followed apace.

Although about 55 percent blue collar, Warren is a relatively affluent city with a median annual family income of about $13,500 in 1970. It is predominantly Polish and Roman Catholic with other large contingents of people of Italian, Canadian, and German parentage.

At the bottom of the rankings of the eight communities--but only by a small margin compared to Pontiac and Warren--Mt. Clemens is the most distant from Detroit lying on the northeastern side of lake St. Clair 25 miles from the city's political boundary. Mount Clemens is the smallest city in the study with just over 20,000 people and a declining population. Although dwarfed in population by its neighbors to the south, St. Clair Shores and Warren, it is the seat of Macomb county by virtue of its being the oldest city in the county (incorporated in 1879). The physical and demographic decline that set in during the past 25 years has not been turned around despite heavy investment in urban renewal in the late fifties. The population in 1970 had declined about 3 percent from the 21,000 of 1960. The $11,000 median annual family income (1970 figures) makes Mount Clemens the second poorest city of the eight in our sample.

The differences described in the sample communities focus on the social patterns of problem helping and represent only one component in a more elaborate methodology for defining quality of life in each locale. We have seen that the strength of helping systems of communities provides a range of differences that may be of significance to the population residing in these communities. The question is, how do these differences affect seniors and retirees? To explore this question let us first of all take a look at some of the neighbor resources that may be available. First of all, the question of watching the house shows that in the strong helping communities there is a 96 percent probability of help. It is in the moderate communities that this probability is lowest, only 57 percent, while it is 69 percent in the low-strength cities. In terms of knowing someone who can help with repairs, both the low-helping-strength as well as the strong community show a higher level than the moderate community.

In regard to dealing with personal problems, 67 percent of seniors residing in strong helping communities report that they have such help from neighbors, compared with only 44 percent for those in low-strength communities.

The differences are as pronounced or consistent "in the collective action" side of neighborhood life. (See Table VIII-2.)

In the "healthy" communities seniors report a greater degree of action helping as well as a particularly strong shift toward referral help for "recent concerns." In addition, "showing a new way to look at a problem" is significantly higher in the strong versus the "medium" and "weak" communities. "Asking question" help also tends to increase. "Listening" help shows a slight opposite trend. In the "healthy" communities, active help and linkage help, that is, referrals, are the major distinguishing characteristics.

Suburban versus Central City Helping Patterns for Seniors

Perhaps one of the most widely discussed topics in urban sociology is the degree to which the central city has been a major source of social contact and the rise of suburban communities seen in terms of their isolated qualities. This theme recently pursued by Fisher (1978) is present in Rosow's (1962) analysis of the aging who find more neighbor contacts in dense urban centers. In the present analysis we shall consider the proposition that the suburban communities surrounding Detroit isolate seniors in a specific way: we shall differences in the development of helping networks as one operational definition of organic solidarity. We refer to the indirect ties that mean in one community there are links to several different kinds of helpers, while in others each person--retiree or senior--has a limited range of helpers.

We shall at this point compare the seniors, age 65 or older who are living within the City of Detroit versus those living in each of the surrounding eight communities which were representatively sampled as part of the core helping network study.[8] Even though there is no difference in the incidence of experiencing recent concerns between suburbs and the central city there is a greater use of at least one helper in Detroit compared to the suburban communities. The figures are 24 percent and 16 percent respectively. While three out of five Detroiters who are seniors have at least two helpers for every recent concern, this is true for only one in three suburban seniors.

Turning to the number of different behaviors that are obtained for each problem, we find that again there is a sharp suburban-Detroit difference. Thus, 55 percent of Detroit seniors receive helping that includes at least three different behaviors compared to only 27 percent for suburban seniors. Thirty percent of the seniors in the suburbs have only one helping behavior for each problem encounter compared to 16 percent with that minimum level among Detroit seniors. (See TABLE VIII-3.)

Is there a difference in the kinds of helpers that are used by Detroit seniors versus those residing in other communities? Spouse-helping in Detroit and the suburban communities is virtually identical. Among Detroit seniors there is more than twice the amount of help from relatives as is found in the suburban communities, while friend-helping is virtually identical in the suburbs compared to Detroit, and neighbor-helping is 38 percent greater in Detroit. Co-workers-helping also occurs at twice the rate in Detroit. Use of formal helpers is also greater for Detroit seniors compared to suburbanities. A substantial part of the increase is due to the use of police in coping with problems. (See Table VIII-4.)

We now turn to the kind of help seniors use for recent concerns. Does this differ between Detroit and its surrounding communities? Detroit seniors report 56 percent of the time that they receive "asking questions" help as compared to only 39 percent in suburban communities. "Listening" help is 21 percent higher in Detroit compared to outlying communities. (See Table VIII-5.)

To further explore indirect social linkages, let us examine several of the resource ties that reflect the local network and the perceptions of the capacity to take action on personal and collective problems. We first note having a neighbor watch over the house when a senior is on vacation is more common in Detroit versus suburban communities. Help with personal problems is also higher in Detroit. Knowing someone in the neighborhood who can do home repairs also is significantly higher in Detroit versus its surrounding communities. In the case of both help with a school principal who is not doing a good job and protesting the local business that is harming the area, the Detroit seniors describe their neighborhoods as far more likely to be capable of action than do suburban seniors. Overall, then, Table VIII-5 has shown that in the areas of collective and individual helping from the neighborhood, resources are greater for Detroit seniors than those living in the surrounding communities.

Well-Being and The Community Factor

We have looked at the degree to which helping networks are more diversified in particular kinds of communities and in terms of the central city-suburban comparison. In "high" helping communities versus "low," the RISK score shifts significantly upward from 9.6 to 13.4. Among seniors those with a higher than average RISK score increased from 46 percent in the "high" helping communities to 59 percent in the low helping communities. The percentage in the upper quartile shows an even greater increase from 23 percent to 40 percent.

In spite of the higher number of problems, (particularly those dealing with crime) that characterize the neighborhoods in Detroit, the well-being of seniors does not show a decline there versus the suburban locals. In fact, we see a slight counter-trend in that the mean Risk-to-well-being score is 14.2 among seniors in the suburban areas compared to 12.4 among Detroit seniors.

One of the explanations that we can offer for the fact that this differential does not occur is to refer back to the differences in the amount and kind of help that is available to seniors in Detroit versus surrounding communities. (See TABLE VIII-6)

Summary

We have found that the differences between central city and suburban areas is a highly significant one in terms of the use of helpers such as neighbors, relatives and formal agencies. The latter difference may indeed reflect the less dense social service network and human service resource in the suburban communities. However, such a structural characteristic can not be used to explain the differences in relative and neighbor helping. It is clear that the informal system as well as the formal system is used to a greater extent by Detroit seniors than by suburban seniors.

We have evidence that the general strength of helping in the sample muncipalities reflects influence on the reported well-being of seniors residing in those particular kinds of environments. The suburban community is a somewhat isolating context for helping persons age 65 or older in our sample. While there are major differences between communities, on a whole, those cities outside of Detroit tend to have weaker networks of help for seniors. The context of social support and particularly instrumental helping is critically shaped by the municipality and by the overall pattern of suburban versus central city locals.

(See TABLE VIII-7)

Without the complex, ramified, indirect, loose-knit ties of the central city, seniors may find themselves relying on a spouse or friends whose significant roles become especially indispensable. In the absence of such help, seniors may not be able to fully participate as both the giver and receiver of help in the variety of contests that may be present in the urban center. In viewing the indirect and organic solidarity of the city as conducive to the social integration of the aging, we, at the same time, must recognize that this can be matched in some cases by a suburban community that is effectively self-contained and supportive in its helping resources. Lack of helping networks may be maximized in a suburb that is homogenous in social composition and yet divided into separate neighborhoods each not linked to the other. Seniors in such settings may be less accessible to the ramified networks of their central city peers. This is not to dispute the fact that a certain degree of "selective recruitment" may operate.

Those seniors who prefer to be less involved in a complex of social ties and who are certainly disturbed by the problems of crime and social diversity that may characterize the urban center are moving toward suburban settings. But this choice often involves movement into a housing pattern or condominium living arrangements in which one is encapsulated in a network of peers of similar age and social background. The effect of this may indeed be a salutary one in terms of personal security, but it also leaves open the question of whether such communities formed by either self-selection or by formal policy produce a kind of ghettoization that we have heard so much about in regard to the life of the senior.

FIGURE 1

MAP OF THE TRI-COUNTY AREAS WITH THE
EIGHT SAMPLE COMMUNITIES

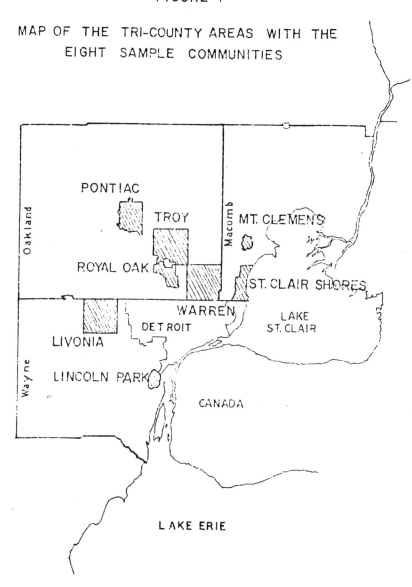

TABLE VIII-1

**Risk to Well Being Score in Relation
to the Eight Municipalities**

	Strength of helping rank
High strength	
Royal Oak	(1)
Lincoln Park	(2)
St. Clair Shores	(3)
Medium strength	
Livonia	(4)
Troy	(5)
Low strength	
Pontiac	(6)
Warren	(7)
Mt. Clemens	(8)

TABLE VIII-2

**Reported and Perceived Mutual Aid in the Local
Neighborhood in Relation to Community Helping
Strength: Persons 65 or Older**

	High strength	Medium strength	Low strength
People keep an eye on each others houses	96%+	57%	69%
There are people who do house or car repairs	15%	7%	18%
People are willing to offer help personal problems	67%+	50%	44%
Neighbors will help do something about a bad school official	30%	31%	29%
Neighbors will organize and protest a business harming the local area	57%+	57%+	36%
	(N=46)	(N=14)	(N=45)

TABLE VIII-3

**Strength of Helping Networks for Seniors in Detroit
Compared to Surrounding Cities**

	Detroit	Surrounding cities
Percent having one or more recent concerns	38%	37%
	(N = 265)	(N = 105)
Number of helpers used for recent concerns:		
None	16%	24%
1	26	40
2	26	19
3	34	16
Total	102%	99%
Number of helping behaviors:		
None	16%	24%
1	16	30
2	13	19
3+	55	27
Total	100%	100%
	(N = 101)	(N = 39)

TABLE VIII-4

Type of Helper Used for Recent Concerns:
Seniors in Detroit Versus Surrounding
Municipalities

	Detroit	Surrounding cities
Spouse	50%	54%
Relative	50%+	21%−
Friend	38%	36%
Neighbor	44%+	32%−
Co-worker	9%+	4%−
Formal helpers:	31%+	21%−
Police	17%+	7%−
Clergy	7%	7%
Doctor	6%	7%
Counselor*	5%+	0%−
Teacher	1%	0%

*

Includes psychiatrist, psychologist, and social worker.

TABLE VIII-5

Type of Helping Behaviors for Seniors
in Detroit Versus Surrounding Cities

	Detroit	Surrounding cities
Listening	94%+	73%−
Asking questions	56%+	32%−
Showing a new way to look at a problem	31%	29%
Referring	25%+	18%−
Taking action	25%	21%
	(N = 101)	(N = 035)

TABLE VIII-6

**Reported and Perceived Mutual Aid in the Local
Neighborhood in Detroit versus Surrounding Cities**

	Detroit	Surrounding cities
People keep an eye on each others	89% +	79% –
There are people who do house or car repairs in the local area	18% +	13% –
People are willing to offer help for personal problems	62% +	55% –
Neighbors will help do something about a bad school official	49% +	30% –
Neighbors will organize and protest a business harming the local area	64% +	47% –

TABLE VIII-7

RISK Score for Persons Age 65 or Older in Relation to Community Helping Strength and City Location

	Percent above median	Percent in upper quartile	Mean score
Strength of community helping:			
high	46%	23%	9.6
medium	50%	29%	12.9
low	59%	40%	13.4
Detroit	48%	30%	12.4
Surrounding cities	52%	30%	14.2

CHAPTER IX

SOCIAL CONTACT AND HELPING: KIN AND FRIENDS

Although R. answered open and freely to my questions, she does not easily make contact with the neighbors, stays much to herself, and relies on her children. Her husband left her many, many years ago when her children were still little to look for work in Chicago, but never came back. He vanished.

R. Said they don't mix with neighbors too much. The family is very close to one another.

R. has a brother with whom she is very close. He is her main source of information. She states that he should have been a politician as he keeps up with everything.

Interviewer Thumbnail Sketches

Up to this point we have devoted considerable attention to only one of the three key forms of informal social ties--neighbors. In the case of family and friends we have two bases of problem coping that are generally more salient, either for the aging or other members of society. When the various helpers for "recent concerns" were initially listed in (see Table IV-2), spouse emerged as the most frequently mentioned helper. While the availability of such an essential social tie declines with age and retirement it is still the most common source of helping for all persons surveyed. We can compare this reliance on spouse helping in terms of two considerations: percent of people with recent concerns who use spouse as a helper and the percent of problems in which help of spouse is sought. In the first instance we are focusing on the probability of *any* help: in the second case it is a matter of the range of help--multiple problem aid.

Our data show the declining availability of spouse helping with retirement coupled with heavy reliance by retirees who have access to such an intimate help. The "diffusion" measure simply shows the difference between help for one problem and help that the same individual receives for multiple "recent concerns." Thus, 61 percent of the time that a problem is experienced by those retired for more than one year, spouse is a helper. This is only 7 percent less than the pattern for persons not approaching retirement. The probability of using spouse at all or of using spouse for several problems by the same individual is highest for those about to retire.

There is a rather precipitious decline in spouse help in the pre-retirement versus immediate post-retirement period. This sudden change may in part be a function of the types of problems encountered after versus before this status change. Partly this pattern results from the smaller proportion of married whites in the post-versus pre-retirement subsamples. (See TABLE IX-1)

What about the kind of spouse help? Does it change with retirement? For example, "just listening" behavior is not as common for those who have been retired for more than a year compared to persons not approaching retirement. "Listening" is at its highest for those who are just about to or who have recently retired. The "asking question" form of helping is high for those who are approaching retirement, but then declines sharply immediately after retirement and then seems to climb once again. Moreover, immediately after retirement, there is a decline in spouse help in terms of "a new way to look at the problem" and the "asking question" form of help. Instead, the spouse in this situation seems to become a focus of "referral" behavior. Upon retirement the spouse is less likely to be a source of help by "taking action" on a recent concern.

The pattern of spouse helping reflects a general narrowing of the range of helping behaviors when retirees have been in their role for at least one year. Particularly noticeable is the reduction in "action" and "referral" helping. Thus, some evidence is presented that the spouse in retirement is more likely to give social support and not action or a new approach to a problem. (See TABLE IX-2)

Kin: Contact and Helping

Let us now turn to the helping role of kin. Table IX-3 shows the frequency of contacts with kin we find that the most frequent contact, that is, measured by reporting visiting with a relative, occurs for those who have just retired. Sixty percent of this group indicate they visit with kin at least once a week. This compares with only 46 percent of those who have been retired for more than a year, and 48 percent for those on the verge of retirement. When we examine the extent to which kin helping occurs for "recent concerns" then we find it is highest among those who have just retired within the past year. A sharp drop occurs for the group retired longer than one year. For both the newly retired and those on the verge of retirement, kin helping for recent concerns is found for half of all such problems. (See Table IX-3)

Table IX-4 examines the extent to which kin helping occurs for recent concerns. Here we note that the percent of people using the relative helping is highest among those who have just retired within the past year. It is lowest for both those who are retired for longer than a year and for those not approaching retirement.

Those persons who are about to retire are the group most likely to use kin helping for recent concerns. But the help appears to be highly specialized since it is used for only 51 percent of all problems encountered by persons on the verge of retirement but 59 percent of the people in this situation. In effect, kin help is not diffused beyond one problem. (See Table IX-4)

Table IX-5 provides information on the particular kind of help that relatives give when sought out for aid. Prior to retirement "asking questions" is the more prevalent pattern in comparison with kin help at other life stages. Just following retirement kin aid takes a form emphasizing listening and referral. For the person who is retired for more than one year both referral and taking action increase vis a vis the immediate post-retirement period.

Let us now turn to the type of help that relatives give when sought out for aid in regard to "recent concerns." "Listening" is most in evidence for those newly retired. Prior to retirement "asking questions" is the more prevalent pattern in comparison with other life stages. "Listening" is the lowest for those retired more than one year. By contrast, both "referral" and "action" help is relatively high. "Asking questions" is particularly evident as a form of help used by those on the verge of retirement.

The variability in emphasis in kin helping may reflect which particular family member is called upon or is available. After retirement there is clearly a key role played by children. This point is stressed in the work of Rosow (1962) and Cantor and Mayer (1977). Patterns shown in Table IX-5 provide a sense of the diversity in helping that the kin system can provide. Overall, the most pronounced shift from pre-to-post retirement status is the heightened role of kin "referral" helping. (See Table IX-5.)

Does the frequency of kin visits affect the well-being of seniors? To evaluate this issue we have correlated the RISK score with the frequency of visiting. Visits of once or twice a week or once or twice a month are correlated with the lowest proportion of seniors who are above the median RISK score. In terms of the upper quadrant of RISK the lowest proportion here occurs for kin visits that are once or twice a week. Our data suggest that lack of kin visiting is detrimental to the well-being of seniors, but that an opposite maximum level of such contact is not an optimal situation either. Part of the explanation for this may lie with the role of helping. Too frequent contact may reflect a multitude of problems. The sociability function of kin ties may suggest a moderate level of visiting is the best balance. (See CHART IX-1)

The Role of Friends

Turning to the network of non-kin intimates we find a general decline in contact based on face-to-face visits after retirement in comparison to other life stages. Our findings indicate that the frequency of friend visits of at least once a week do not undergo a major shift based on retirement. The decline is a very modest one--toward bi-monthly rather than bi-weekly visits. (See Table IX-6.)

For "recent concern" helping the decline in aid for persons retired longer than one year is greater than the modest shift in fact-to-face visiting might suggest. At the same time, the high rate of using friend help just before retirement is not predicted by the virtually identical frequency of friend visits of those two groups in the survey. Does the slight decline in the frequency also predict a similar reduction in the use of friends for problem coping? The probability of friend helping for recent concerns is greatest just prior to retirement. Thereafter it declines, but drops especially far for those retired longer than one year--to 28 percent. Yet this same group appears to have a number of recent concerns. This is a narrowing of those who use friends yet a widening range of problems are implicated. (See TABLE IX-7)

In regard to "life crisis" helping we find no substantial shift based on life cycle and retirement. Given the decline in "recent concern" helping for persons retired for over one year, the role of friend for this group comes increasingly to be that of a life crisis helper. For other groups there is a more equal role for friend aid.

Does the kind of help friends offer for recent concerns shift with life stage? We find that "listening" help is especially common for persons who have been retired for more than one year, while "showing a new way" to look at a concern is especially high among persons who have retired within the last year. For persons approaching retirement and those who have already become retired, we find that referral helping is less prevalent in comparison to those at other life stages. (See TABLE IX-8)

Summary

The social contact with kin and friends and the helping patterns of spouse, relatives and friends suggest both general similarities and several unique configurations. Not surprisingly, kin are visited with more frequency than friends. Moreover, the period immediately following retirement is associated with even more contact and helping sought from relatives than either before or after this "passage." Friend contact declines in frequency with retirement--that is face-to-face interaction. The spouse tends to become more of a socially supportive helper once retirement occurs rather than an instrumental helper. They also engage heavily in referral helping.

Help seeking from friends along with that of spouse appears to be used for a wider variety of recent concerns for persons retired for more than a year. This pattern of more intensive use of primary group helper by a smaller proportion of the people experiencing concerns is not as prevalent in regard to kin help. Because of the single indicator of social contact--face-to-face visits--our analysis of the link between helping and primary group ties is a limited one. Use of telephone contact, for example, was not included in the survey. The findings that are available are nevertheless suggestive of the co-equal role shared by kin, friends, and spouse for the retired. This greater apparent interchangeability with retirement can only be suggested by the data we have reviewed. In the next chapter we shall explore this issue in greater depth.

TABLE IX-1

Extent of Spouse Helping for Recent Concerns

	Retired more than 1 year before interview	Retired within the last year	To retire within 1 year after interview	Other persons inter- viewed
Percent of persons with one or more recent concerns using spouse helping	44%	39%	70%	64%
Percent of all recent concerns where spouse is used as a helper	61%	37%	76%	68%
Diffusion*	+17%	−2%	+6%	+4%

*Extent to which percent of persons using a given helper matches frequency of helper use for recent concerns. A "+" denotes that spouse is being used for more than one problem per user.

TABLE IX-2

Type of Help Provided by Spouse for Recent Concerns

	Retired more than 1 year before interview	Retired within the last year	To retire within 1 year after interview	Other persons inter-viewed
Listening	87%−	100%+	100%+	83%
Asking questions	48%	22%−	64%+	56%
Showing a new way to look at the problem	21%	16%	26%	28%
referring	9%	22%+	5%−	11%
Taking action	9%−	11%−	16%	21%

TABLE IX-3

Frequency of Visiting with Relatives

	Retired more than 1 year before interview	Retired within the last year	To retire within 1 year after interview	Other persons inter-viewed
Almost every day	6%	28%+	10%	8%
Once or twice a week	40	32	38	39
Once or twice a month	29	22	38	31
A few times a year or less	21	17	15	20
Never	4	2	0	2
TOTAL %	100%	101%	101%	100
	(N=275)	(N=054)	(N=040)	(N=)

TABLE IX-4

Extent of Kin Helping for Recent Concerns
and Life Crises

	Retired more than 1 year before interview	Retired within the last year	To retire within 1 year after interview	Other persons inter- viewed
Percent of persons with one or more recent concerns using relative helping	28%	59%	48%	38%
Percent of all recent concerns where relative is used as a helper	34%	51%	49%	32%
Diffusion*	+6%	−8%	+1%	−6%
Kin help for life crises#	83%	82%	79%	77%

*Extent to which percent of persons using a given helper matches frequency of helper use for recent concerns. A "+" denotes that relative is being used for more than one problem per user.

#Includes spouse.

TABLE IX-4

Type of Help Provided by Relatives for Recent Concerns

	Retired more than 1 year before interview	Retired within the last year	To retire within 1 year after interview	Other persons inter-viewed
Listening	66%−	86%+	77%	79%
Asking questions	47%	37%−	69%+	51%
Showing a new way to look at the problem +	15%	14%	8%−	25%
Referring −	39%+	29%+	15%−	12%
Taking action −	18%+	0%−	15%+	8%

TABLE IX-6

Frequency of Visiting with Friends

	Retired more than 1 year before interview	Retired within the last year	To retire within 1 year after interview	Other persons inter-viewed
Almost every day	2%	8%	3%	3%
Once or twice a week	25	25	30	30
Once or twice a month	35	36	45	42
A few times a year or less	29	23	18	22
Never	9	9	5	4
TOTAL	100%	101%	101%	101%

TABLE IX-7

**Extent of Friend Helping for Recent Concerns
and Life Crises**

	Retired more than 1 year before interview	Retired within the last year	To retire within 1 year after interview	Other persons inter-viewed
Percent of persons with one or more recent concerns using friend helping	28%	43%	52%	42%
Percent of all recent concerns where friend is used as a helper	38%	37%	43%	40%
Diffusion*	+10%	−6%	−9%	−2%
Friend help for life crises	58%	64%	55%	61%

*Extent to which percent of persons using a given helper matches frequency per use for recent concerns. A "+" denotes friend is being used for more than one problem per user.

TABLE IX-8

Type of Help Provided by Friend for Recent Concerns

	Retired more than 1 year before interview	Retired within the last year	To retire within 1 year after interview	Other persons inter- viewed
Listening	93%+	78%	79%	85%
Asking questions	45%	38%−	50%	53%
Showing a new way to look at the problem +	22%	49%+	14%	22%
Referring +	15%	10%	14%	22%
Taking action	7%	0%	7%	8%

CHART IX-1

Frequency of Visits with Relatives and RISK
Score for Persons 65 or older

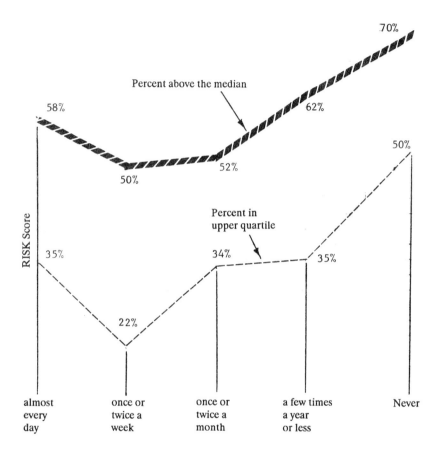

CHAPTER X

HELPING NETWORKS AND THE FUNCTIONAL SPECIALIZATION OF INFORMAL HELPERS

The couple seem to "keep to themselves." R. was very surprised and delighted to have been helped by a friend of a neighbor who fixed their color TV set for them.

This is a lonely widow who tries to get along without much help from her children and others. She has had many bad experiences with neighbors next door harassing her. Three teenagers were on her porch at 1:00 A.M. one night. They attempted to break in, threw snowballs at her house, etc. The police said, 'Lady, what can we do?' A man dumped black dirt on her lawn and demanded $75.00 for it. She paid it, but called the police. They didn't help. The Allstate Insurance Company agent got a Lincoln Park policeman to help. Her daughter called the police. They said, 'Tell your mother she is stupid as can be.' So Mrs. V. took action herself and traced the owner of the truck company, but he had moved.

Interviewer Thumbnail Sketches

In this chapter we shall consider several major theoretical issues in the understanding of how kin, friends, and neighbors play a role in the life of the elderly. In particular, we shall refer to work carried out by several researchers and then go on to consider a set of findings drawn from the database of the helping network study. Some conclusions will drawn about the implications of the analysis in terms of the extant literature.

Some Research Perspectives on Aging and Informal Social Ties

In the major study by Rosow--*Social Interaction of the Aged*--a concept is posited that loyalties between family, friends and neighbors are competitive and tend to be mutually exclusive. Rosow (1962:166) suggests that researchers "should try to analyze all three groups on relatively neutral ground where they can fully compete with each other on fairly equal terms without the constraints of functional inappropriateness or major cultural imperatives." Rosow further asks "How salient are they (friends, kin, neighbors) as free reference groups outside the spheres of family responsibility and age role models?" He concludes that neighbors can challenge the role of family but friends cannot: "In cases of high role loss, such as might occur through retirement or bereavement, the high residential density of older people afforded greater opportunities for replacing friends (with neighbors)."

A more recent elaboration of the theme of the separation in functions among informal helpers is developed by Eugene Litwak and his colleagues (1978, 1986). This research stresses the importance of delineating the conceptual attributes of particular tasks that are performed by various helpers:

> The argument that groups with different structures perform the same tasks further assumes tat tasks do not vary in terms of the group dimensions they require. Such an assumption is rejected on face validity grounds. For instance, the following tasks require individuals to live in close physical proximity to the older person: spotting a burglary when the resident has gone shopping, keeping a visual check on a frail elderly person to make sure he or she has not had an accident. . . or obtaining information on which storekeepers in the neighborhood are helpful to older people. A person who lives in a different neighborhood or a different block is much less likely to provide these services on a continuing basis . . . (*Dono, Litwak*, et al., 1978, p. 30)

Kin, friendship and neighbor helping is distinguished in terms of the key dimensions of long-term commitment versus physical proximity:

On the other hand some tasks require primary group ties that involve long term commitments but not necessarily . . . close proximity. For instance, an older person may get considerable comfort and advice over the phone on their relation to their children or kin, their financial affairs or making plans to have their home looked after if they are going on vacation or to the hospital.

(*Ibid.*)

This theoretical perspective marks a distinction between the preferred helper such as kin who may not be available and neighbors who substitute as "the effective unit" of helping. The theory of functional specificity of primary groups (informal helpers) predicts which groups can be most effective in handling what particular kind of task (Litwak and Szelenyi, 1970). Thus, the question of tasks sampled is not simply a methodological one but has critical meaning for the underlying conceptual schema. If, inadvertently, a researcher uses tasks that consistently require physical proximity to be carried out, then the result would show a particular helper as the most preferred.

In her research on neighbors and friends social support, Marjorie Cantor addresses some of the key issues that Litwak focuses on in discussing the primary groups of the aging in urban society. By noting a form of "behavioral blurring," Cantor sees less basic importance in distinguishing the roles of friends and neighbors in the life of the elderly. Robert Kahn (1978) has also addressed the issues of what kind of helpers the aging person utilizes. He focuses on a concept of the "life course convoy"--a perspective in which different helpers are drawn upon at different key stages of a persons life. A set of informal helpers must be situationally defined rather than seen in terms of invariant functions.

"Recent Concerns" and the Question of Functional Specialization

The approach in the helping network study permits some testing of the theoretical perspectives we have briefly reviewed. We would argue, for example, that the set of recent concerns are "non-uniform" versus "uniform tasks" in the sense that Litwak has utilized a dichotomy that identifies underlying attributes of problems which can or cannot be divided into discrete and uniform parts. Moreover, the attributes of long-term commitment versus physical proximity which Litwak sees as basic to the division of labor between friend/kin versus neighbor help are not clearly required. While such "life crises" as those defined by Holmes and Rahe may heave "uniform" elements of one-time help, the recent concerns may entail repeated advice and decision making contact that involves unique combinations of asking questions, referring, or taking some action.

In the present analysis we shall examine the way in which friend, kin, and neighbor helping for recent concerns (and life crises) may involve specialization as to who is a helper, what they do to help, and how both of these aspects of informal aid may change with time and retirement status. The character of the recent concern list as well as the kind of data on what form of help is provided may fulfill the need for a "neutral" basis that Rosow argues is needed to evaluate the competing roles of different primary groups. At the same time, the type of approach outlined by Kahn can be addressed because of the comparison of people just before, after, and still farther into a retirement status.

When we speak about the "functional roles" of the various primary or informal helpers, we can approach this in several ways. First we can say, given a similar problem, that it is more likely that that problem will be handled by a variety of different support helpers. And, if this occurs more often for those who are retired, this can serve is evidence of a "functional substitutability can." However, if we find that upon retirement no increase in the sharing of helping for the same type of problem occurs, this can offer evidence in support of the notion of the "functionally specific" or "task specific role" of each kind of helping resource. The latter, would be more supportive of the Litwak formulation.

Problem-Specific Differentiation of Helpers.

We approach the general analytical question by selecting the two neighborhood problems and the two mood problems which provide a way to examine, in the first instance, whether the help of neighbors tends to predominate mo with the retired person or not. We begin our empirical analysis by considering the extent to which kin, friends, and neighbors are each used by the retired and non-retired for coping with "recent concerns." To round out the analysis, we must also consider the role of spouse--his or her absence is key. Spouse helping has declined with retirement, while friend and kin helping show no significant changes by retirement status. However, neighbor help is almost doubled for the retired compared to the non-retired in our sample. (see Table X-1).

For both of the neighborhood-related problems, there is no significant difference between the probability of neighbor help in comparison with help from spouse, relatives or friends. There is a slight tendency for neighbor help, in fact, to be somewhat greater in the instance of fear of crime for those who have not retired. For the two mood-related problems, we find that there is an increase in the use of the neighbor in comparison with the other primary group helpers. Both of these differences are fairly large in scale, suggesting that neighbor help seems to be spreading beyond simply neighborhood problems. (See TABLE X-2)

Let us now consider the range of use of one helper, that is, which helper tends to be used the most and which the least for a specific problem. We find some differences between the retired and non-retired respondents in the survey. For three out of the four problems where there is a fairly wide use of several different kinds of helpers we find that the retired group is less likely to show a larger range between the various helpers for a given problem. In other words, there is more likely to be a distribution of use of all helpers on a more equal basis. There is one problem in which this is not the case: the decision to move from the neighborhood. We find a heavy use by the retired of kin to consider this problem, whereas the spouse is used for non-retired persons. Such a shift suggests a substitutability once retirement status is attained. (See Appendix Table X-1.)

We have summarized the functional substitutability of helpers by taking the range of differences between the maximum use of a particular helper and the minimum use of a different helper. This "range" suggests to what degree there is a concentration of the use of one particular helper to the exclusion of the other three. When we carry out this analysis for "recent concerns" we find that the range is minimized for those who have been retired for more than a year-16 percent. It is 25 percent for those newly retired; 41 percent for those who will retire within a year.

If we look at "life crises," we find that there is a significant shift in the degree to which one informal helper is relied on to the exclusion of others. The discrepancy tends to be lowest for those who have recently retired but overall the pattern suggests no great difference. At the same time, when the friend-neighbor pairing is examined, we see a similar pattern to that noted for "recent concerns." This implies that friend-neighbor helping becomes more equal as we move from persons not approaching retirement to those who have been retired for more than a year.

Our data suggest that functional specialization among helpers tends to be weakened with retirement and that a greater probability of interchangeability or substitutability of helpers does tend to occur in coping with "recent concern" helping. The nature of these "low invoked expertise" problems permits a degree of shift in who can provide help, that is, who is sought for help for a specific problem. Moreover this pattern also is one in which is not only a shift away from the more exclusive reliance on a particular helper for one particular problem, but that the use of a given helper decreases significantly in most instances as one goes from a non-retirement to a retirement status. (See TABLE X-3)

Functional Specialization in the Kind of Help Provided

Now we can turn to the question of whether the particular *content* of the helping transaction shows that what a given helper does for an individual in regard to a particular problem may also become interchangeable in terms of the different kinds of primary group helpers that may be utilized or whether it remains relatively functionally specific to a particular helper

We will now examine the degree to which different helpers are more likely to use the same type of help at different stages of the retirement "passage." In terms of spouse helping for "recent concerns," there is a shift from "action" in the pre-retirement categories to other kinds of help after retirement. "Listening" and "asking" behavior are high just before retirement (the latter tends to decline immediately after retirement). "Referral" helping is on high just after retirement. For relative helping, listening behavior is high just after retirement and then declines; asking questions is high just before and also declines immediately after retirement. "Showing a new way to look at a problem" is particularly high for those not approaching retirement, and then declines. "Referral" help is higher after retirement and remains high; taking "action" helping is high, but not before or just after retirement; it further declines when a person has been retired for more than a year. In the case of friend helping, "referral" and asking "question" help is higher before rather than after retirement. For neighbor helping, "listening" and "asking" is more common for individuals on the verge of retirement and then shifts to a "referral" emphasis after retirement.

A functional indicator of the number of times a given helper shows a changed helping behavior emphasis in provided in Table X-4. Since there are four groups and five types of help utilized (see Appendix Table X-2) a total of twenty possible shifts can occur. Kin helping shows the most frequent change in emphasis--13 out of a possible 20 times a change occurs. Neighbor help shows 9 and spouse help 8 shifts. Friend helping is least "flexible"--it shows only 3 shifts out of a possible 20. The changing emphases of particular helpers provides one measure of the presence or absence of sharp functional specialization of primary group helpers. Our data suggest that--for recent concerns--kin, neighbors, and spouse are less specialized than friends. (See TABLE X-4)

Does the kind of problem influence changing content for given helpers? Here we can examine the patterns for "life crises" in comparison with that of "recent concerns." We had initially conceptualized the former problems as less "nonuniform." Overall, we find that a smaller number of shifts in type of help occur compared to "recent concern" helping. Kin help, as in the case of "recent concerns," shows more flexibility--more changes in emphasis. Yet the direction is not reversed. For "life crises" helping, kin take action relatively more after retirement than before, whereas the reverse was true for "recent concerns." However, referral help goes up after retirement in the case of both crises and concerns. (See Tables X-5 & 6).

Helping versus Social Contact

As we have noted earlier, a major theoretical consideration in the helping-network study is to point out the conceptual distinction between helping behavior and social contact. We have also distinguished helping behaviors as "social support" versus "instrumental helping." Since we do have measures of sociability between relatives, friends and neighbors as distinct from their use as helpers, we can specifically test out the conceptual model of the relative independence of these two processes or functions. One way to carry out this analysis is to examine the percentage of helping that is independent of face-to-face visiting. In the case of relatives we find that the absence of visiting virtually seems to exclude the possibility of help for "recent concerns." This is partially the case for friend helping which is 17 percent where there is no face-to-face visit. In contrast, neighbor helping without visiting is quite high: 40 percent. (See TABLE X-7)

The second indicator of the independence of social contact from helping in the neighborhood, in the family and in the friendship network is to correlate the amount of help given when people report that they have no close friends in each of these behavior arenas. In the case of both friends and relatives, without having at least one person who is seen to be a person who is a close friend, there is no help. However, in the case of neighbors, there is a 27 percent helping rate where there is no close friend in the locale. These findings tend to underscore the dual character of the neighborhood: it has social contacts which are often the basis of helping, but at the same time, can provide helping which is not dependent on social closeness.

The relationships between "sociability" and "helping" are based upon face-to-face visiting. This was the only measure available in the interview instrument. One could then argue that without measuring telephone communication, there is a serious limitation on the findings we have noted. Moreover, neighbor contacts based on casual meetings on the street are also excluded from the present analysis. It is perfectly valid to point out that the presence of neighbor and some friend help in the absence of face-to-face visits means that such help could come via non-face-to-face telephone or casual talking. Yet this point, rather than necessarily challenging the meaning of our findings further reinforces them. For it is precisely because the neighborhood and the friendship arena may contain "loose-knit" or casual, occasional ties that we can see the diverse way in which helping networks develop.

Let us further examine the relationship between social closeness and help for recent concerns we can comparing persons under age 65 versus over age 65 who have visits or who have close friends among persons living in the neighborhood, among relatives, and among those who are friends Living outside of the neighborhood or beyond the metropolitan area. In the case of persons 65 years and older, there is a pattern of friend closeness being correlated with helping. This pattern is not present for those who are under 65. Thus, we have a reversal of neighbor correlation in the sense that seniors who use friends for helping are also those who report more close friends.

When we turn to kin helping, the pattern is a combination of that found for neighbor and friend. First of all, in regard to the frequency of face-to-face visiting, kin help tends to depend much more on this contact for seniors. There is no relationship between the number of relatives who are considered close friends and helping for seniors. There is a moderate correlation in this regard for those who are under age 65. (See TABLE X-8)

Inferring Cause and Effect Between Helping and Sociability

While we can only indirectly investigate the question of whether helping stimulates social intimacy or the reverse, several indicators can be devised to offer hints about this issue. In particular it is important to ask whether the retired or aging in our society seek help to find sociability, or find sociability as a result of seeking help for problems. Graves (1979) investigated this question using the present study but did so for the entire sample and did not separate seniors from others. For our present purposes we need to compare each group to ascertain if the same dynamic applies to both.

Let us examine the correlation of help in the first year of interviewing with help in the follow-up interviews as shown for each of the different types of primary group helpers, including spouse. (See Table X-9.) The table shows the correlations in terms of those age 65 or older or those under age 65. We find some rather clear-cut patterns. First, the fact is that help from a neighbor at one time is very highly correlated with help from the neighbor in follow-up. This is also true of the spouse. Both show that help for seniors is highly correlated with earlier help. This is less likely to be the case for those under age 65.

Using a spouse for help at one time is not as likely to lead to such help in the next instance, except as one has attained age 65. In regard to kin helping a similar pattern prevails. While the correlation is not a strong one, there tends to be somewhat of a reverse or negative relationship for those under 65. That is, there is some tendency for relative help, when used once, not to be used again. In the case of friend helping, we find a reversal in the sense that help once being correlated with help again is more likely to be the case for those who are under age 65 rather than who have attained that age. Thus, for seniors, friend helping in one case is independent of whether the friend will be used again. (See TABLE X-9)

We can also directly examine the question of whether social contact in one year is associated with help in the next year. Gamma correlations are used in regard to frequency of contact with neighbors, relatives and friends and help from each of these kinds of primary groups in 1975 and one year later. The relationship is a correlation for neighbor helping is significant. That is, if one has been in visiting contact with the neighbor in the earlier year, this is associated with help in the following year. This is not the case for relatives or friends. That is, to say help does not seem to rely on face-to-face socializing. In the case of closeness, we see that help which is given in 1974 does not correlate with the increasing number of persons in the neighborhood who are seen as close friends. However, help from friends is correlated with the number or the size of friendship networks especially in the metropolitan area. (See TABLE X-10)

Some Conceptual Interpretations

We find that both kin and friend helping is initially dependent on a high frequency of face-to-face contact. We can interpret this to mean that instrumental helping must be built into frequent social interaction so as not to "overload" the relationship. Thus, help in 1974 is positively correlated in both instances with a current high degree of visiting. By contrast, neighbor help is uncorrelated with such contact. However, subsequent helps--(longer term or repeated helping) is correlated with frequent face-to-face visiting. All of this represents the pattern for seniors. In the case of non-seniors, kin, friend and neighbor help all depend to some degree on frequent face-to-face contact. These relationships appear to be subject to an "equilibrium" principle. There is a slight indication--because of the somewhat lower correlation--that kin helping is less affected by such a principle.

Seniors and non-seniors alike cannot afford to overload friendship ties in the shortrun. Since these same relationships may be seen as relatively permanent though, it is likely that, in the long run, one can go back to a friend repeatedly or continuously. Thus, we find that friend help in one year is not correlated with friend help in the next. While we have no direct data on whether it is the same individual friends, our data suggest that for older respondents in our sample help is not associated with the growth of friendship networks. For seniors, helping appears to "build" friendship social networks. Thus size of friend network in 1975 is correlated positively ($+26$ and $+.15$) with 1974 friend helping. No similar correlations occur for non-seniors.

In the case of kin neither non-seniors nor seniors appear to be able to build closeness as a result of help seeking. Help from kin in one year is correlated with help the next. If we then assume that the help in the latter instance is coming form the same "base" of kin helpers, this means that seniors can repeatedly seek help without damaging kin social ties. This may indeed be an operational definition of a kin social network. Were friends or neighbors to function in this same fashion, they too could qualify as "quasi-family."

For both seniors and nonseniors the help of neighbors appears to depend in a longer-run sense on earlier face-to-face contact with neighbors. In the case of seniors, however, such dependency is not present for short run help.

Many seniors report having no visits with neighbors and no neighbors who are close friends, yet use neighbors for "recent concern" helping. This also occurs for non-seniors, but to a far lesser extent. Neighborhood is a social arena with two kinds of resources: acquaintances or non-intimates and

184

neighborhood friends. Help from the "neighborhood" is not initially dependent on frequent face-to-face visits with local intimates. Yet, help from the "neighborhood" is sustainable without the "overload" problem of friendships if non-repeated helping can be based on contact with "loose knit," non-friend neighbors. Thus, that in our data, the help for seniors is sustained from 1974 to 1975 by a mixture of using proximate friends in the neighborhood and using acquaintances or possibly referred friends of neighborhood friends.

For seniors and non-seniors alike, long-term neighbor help is dependent upon some face-to-face visiting with local friends. While there is evidence that non-seniors can build neighborhood friendships as a product of helping, seniors appear not to do so. The size of close friendships in the neighborhood is not increased for seniors because of using neighbor help. At first, seniors may use a wide mixture of intimates and non-initimates in the neighborhood for help. But over the longer pull, the non-initimates cannot be used for repeated help--only the closer friends. Thus after initially not depending on sociability, neighbor help does require a degree of social closeness.

Summary

Let us now review the findings in regard to functional specialization among primary group helpers. For "recent concerns" we find that there are frequent shifts in what a given helper tends to do depending on the retirement stage. A concept of "matching" can be used to describe how much one particular helper will emerge as dominant or central at one state in the retirement sequence. By discussing both "matching" and "helping behaviors" an overall picture of functional specialization can be drawn. Matching of several helpers at the same stage of life or shifts in the cluster of helping behaviors both are found to be less pronounced for "life crises" compared to "recent concerns." Therefore, our findings reflect the fact that the latter events appear to maximize the probability that low functional specialization will occur between kin, friends and neighbors in providing for the retired and aging segments of our society.

We have reviewed several ways in which to consider the functional specialization that may occur between friends, neighbors and relatives and particularly how this might be more true for seniors or retired persons versus other individuals in society. Our findings have tended to support the concept of a high degree of interchangeability between the helpers. Clearly, the trends we have noted in this chapter reflect a particular selection of problems. No across-the-board conclusion ought to be developed which denies a high degree of specialization for different kinds of primary group social resources.

Finally, we have found evidence that a functional specialization occurs *within* social ties. That "helping" on the one hand and "sociability" on the other are not coterminous. Sociability provides the possibility of help, but it can also "overload" friendship networks. While this is perhaps less true for kin ties, it does suggest a limit that may be reached for a particular type of primary group tie.

TABLE X-1

**Recent Concern Helping by Spouse, Kin, Friends
and Neighbors for Retired and Non-Retired**

	Percent of all concerns where helper is used	
	All retired persons	Non-retired persons
Spouse	60% –	71% +
Kin	42%	39%
Friends	39%	40%
Neighbors	37% +	20% –

TABLE X-2

Helpers Used for Specific Recent Concerns:
Retired Versus Non-Retired
Persons

		Retired	Non-retired
Crime in the local neighborhood	spouse	−	+
	relative		
	friend	+	−
	neighbor	−	+
Thinking about moving because of crime	spouse		
	relative	+	
	friend	−	+
	neighbor		
Feel like "it's no use trying to do things"	spouse	−	+
	relative	+	−
	friend		
	neighbor	+	−
Feel so "low" it ruined your whole day	spouse		
	relative		
	friend	−	+
	neighbor	+	−

TABLE X-3

**Interchangeability of Informal Helpers for Recent
Concerns and Life Crises: Four Retirement
Groups**

	Retired more than 1 year before interview	Retired within the last year	To retire within 1 year after interview	Other persons inter- viewed

Recent Concerns

Range:

Kin, friend, neighbor	0%	18%	27%	15%
Friend- neighbor	0%	2%	27%	15%
Kin-friend	0%	16%	4%	4%
Kin-neighbor	0%	18%	23%	11%
Spouse- relative vs. friend- neighbor	16%	25%	41%	33%

Life Crises

Range:

Kin, friend, neighbor	32%	27%	35%	29%
Friend- neighbor	4%	9%	11%	13%
Kin-friend	28%	18%	24%	16%
Kin-neighbor	32%	27%	35%	29%
Relative vs. friend- neighbor	23%	0%	20%	32%

TABLE X-4

**Changing Patterns of What Helpers Do for Recent
Concerns in Relation to Retirement**

Spouse:

8/20 shifts

More "taking action" before versus after retirement.

Highest "listening" and "asking question" just before retirement.

Referring high just after retirement.

Relative:

13/20 shifts

"Taking action" declines steadily as retirement approaches and is lowest when it has occured over one year earlier.

"Listening" is high just after retirement and then declines.

"Asking questions" is high just before and then drops to the lowest level immediately after.

"Showing a new way" is high but drops just before retirement.

Referral goes up right after retirement and stays high.

Friend:

3/20 shifts

Referring and asking questions is high up to the time of retirement and then declines.

Showing a new way to look at a problem is high right after retirement.

Neighbor:

9/20 shifts

Listening is high just before retirement.

Asking questions remains high up to retirement, and sharply declines right after.

Taking action is low right after retirement.

Referral is low just before retirement and then sharply rises right after and continues at an even higher level later.

TABLE X-5

Changing Patterns of What Helpers Do
for Life Crises in Relation to Retirement

Relatives (includes spouse):

	More taking action for persons retired more than one year, less immediately after retirement.
5/20 shifts	More referral right after retirement and less "just listen" help.
	More "asking questions" and "showing a new way" right after retirement than at other times.

Friends:

	Highest referral and "asking questions" right after retirement.
3/20 shifts	"Showing a new way" to look at a problem highest just before retirement.

Neighbors:

	Lowest "listening" and "showing a new way" but highest referral helping right after.
3/20 shifts	Lowest "asking questions" help for those retired for more than one year.

TABLE X-6

Match in Who Helps and How
They Help for Recent Concerns

Recent Concerns

+ − Spouse-relative: steady increase in matching of both helpers, but type of helping increasingly does not match

− + Spouse-friend: greatest matching right after retirement; least matching in type of help just before and after retirement; then highest matching for those retired more than 1 year

+ − Spouse-neighbor: matching of who helps highest right after retirement but type of help least matched at this point, then increases back to earlier levels for those retired 1 year or more

+ − Relative-friend: high matching declines just after retirement, then reaches highest level later; matching declines after retirement

+ − Relative-neighbor: matching drops just before and after retirement, then reaches highest point; type of help match declines starting with pre-retirement

+ + Neighbor-friend: highest matching once retirement occurs, lowest just before; type of help matching highest for those retired 1 year or more; lowest for pre-and post-retirement stage

+ − Spouse-kin versus friend-neighbor: matching of who helps greatest for those retired at least one year, steady increase from lowest matching just before retirement; least type of help matching just after retirement, increase to pre-retirement level occurs for those retired 1 year or more

+ − Range-relative, friend, neighbor: highest for those retired for more than 1 year; lowest for those nearing retirement; type of help matching is lowest for those newly retired, increases for those retired longer but is not greater than those about to retire

TABLE X-7

Help Without Social Interaction and Closeness: Persons age 65 or Older

| | Percent of persons with one or more recent concerns | |
	Never visit	No close friends
Relative help	0%	0%
Friend help	17%	0%[*]
		17%[#]
Neighbor help	40%	27%

[*] Friends who live within the metropolitan area
[#] Friends who live outside of the metropolitan area

TABLE X-8

Helping and Sociability:
Seniors and Non-Seniors

	Age 65 or more	Under age 65
Frequency of visits and neighbor help (1974)	$g = +.00$	$g = +.30$ [*]
Number of neighbors as close friends and neighbor help (1975)	$g = +.01$	$g = +.36$ [*]
Frequency of visits and kin help (1974)	$g = +.28$ [*]	$g = +.10$
Number of relatives as close friends and relative help (1975)	$g = +.02$	$g = +.15$
Frequency of visits and friend help (1974)	$g = +.30$ [*]	$g = +.20$ [*]
Number of close friends in the metro area and friend help (1975)	$g = +.38$ [*]	$g = +.02$
Number of close friends outside the metro area and friend help (1975)	$g = +.29$ [*]	$g = +.01$

[*]g = gamma values.

TABLE X-9

**Correlation of 1974-75 Helping for Informal
Helpers: Seniors and Non-Seniors**

	Age 65 or more	Age under 65
Neighbor help: 1974-75	$g = +.73^{*}$	$g = +.20^{*}$
Spouse help: 1974-75	$g = +.70^{*}$	$g = +.15$
Kin help: 1974-75	$g = +.33^{*}$	$g = -.12$
Friend help: 1974-75	$g = +.07$	$g = +.23^{*}$

*Asterisk indicates coefficient is significant at .05 or beyond

TABLE X-10

**Help Leading to Sociability and the
Opposite: Seniors and Non-Seniors**

	Age 65 or older	Under 65
1974 recent concern helping and 1975 number of close friends:		
neighbors	$g = +.05$	$g = +.10$
relative	$g = -.02$	$g = +.03$
friend:		
a) in metro area	$g = +.26^*$	$g = +.02$
b) beyond metro area	$g = +.15$	$g = +.01$
1974 frequency of visiting and 1975 helping for recent concerns		
neighbor help	$g = +.22^*$	$g = +.20^*$
relative help	$g = +.04$	$g = +.14$
friend help	$g = +.01$	$g = +.09$

CHAPTER XI

AGING AND RETIREMENT: SOCIAL INTEGRATION PATTERNS

Mr. Garrett was keenly interested in politics and upon completion of the interview wanted me to spend a few minutes discussing the political situation and the forthcoming gubernatorial primary. From his responses to the questions, he appeared to be very resourceful and competent. When asked what he liked best about his neighborhood, he stated: 'Well, I like people. I'm a bachelor and if I moved to some residential area I wouldn't have people contact. As it is, everytime I step out the door there is a neighborhood friendliness.'

R. was friendly, but insisted he didn't 'have any opinions worth giving.' He wanted to have his wife interviewed instead. As the interview went on he relaxed more and talked more freely. Although he is not active now, he was very active in a senior citizen's group and in his lodge and kept up with the community groups and problems until a year ago or so.

When asked what things she likes least about her neighborhood, she said, 'Just living with all old age people. It's depressing at times, with deaths, illnesses, and the problems of the aged.'

Interviewer Thumbnail Sketches

The theme of social isolation and retreat from major social roles is, of course, a major one dominating the literature, both theoretical and descriptive in regard to aging and retirement. There are a variety of theories describing this process of the separation of the individual from society. In previous chapters we have identified a number of characteristics of the helping process which reflect patterns of isolation and restricted access to the helping of those who have become retired. In this present chapter we will focus on the overall pattern of social contact in terms of both primary group and organizational ties.

Primary Group Contacts

Let us first focus our attention on the informal social ties of kin, friends and neighbors. By summing the three types of social ties we obtain a picture of the total volume of face-to-face visiting that occurs. Persons retired for more than a year are least likely to have a high volume of once-a-week visiting and most likely to have no visiting at all. The ratio is about two to one of once a week versus no contact. By contrast, those newly retired and persons on the verge of retirement show slightly less frequent contact. Those nearing retirement status closely resemble those that are newly retired: a high level of weekly contact and a relatively low level of no contact. (See TABLE XI-1)

We also can compare numbers of reported contact persons for each of the three kinds of informal ties: relatives, neighbors and friends living outside of the neighborhood. Summing across these kinds of informal social contacts (including the two types of friends), we find that those on the verge of retirement have the highest average (14.3) among the various informal groupings. This declines to 12.2 for those newly retired and to a low point of 9.0 for those that have been retired for longer than a year. Thus, we find that for the newly retired there is an increase in the frequency of contact with friends, neighbors and relatives, but not an increase in the number of close friends among those groups. We could view this as another indication of the relatively limited potential that social contacts for retired are able to generate. (See Table XI-2.)

We find that co-worker friendships decline very sharply at the time of retirement. However, there is also a very sharp decline in the average number of friends who are located in the neighborhood. This tends to rebound somewhat for those who are retired for longer than a year. Such a recovery, however, is not seen for relatives who are close friends or for friends in the metropolitian area or beyond. There is a significant increase at the time of retirement in friends in the metropolitan area.

Those who are on the verge of retirement tend to have the highest number of close friends in the widest range of primary group or informal group settings. They have the highest average number of neighbor friends, co-worker friends, and relative friends. They also are likely to have the highest number of friends who live outside the metropolitan area. At the time of retirement, there is an increase in the number of friends in the metropolitan area and a decline in all other categories. Once the individual has been retired for longer than a year, there is a decline in friends outside of the metropolitan area and a stabilization of the size of friendship of those in the metropolitan area, coupled with a decline in co-worker close friendships.

Retirement: Changing Needs or Change of Personality?

The theme of the personality changes that occur when an individual enters upon retirement status represents a major area of research and theory. In the present study we do not have elaborate measures of personality, but several questions based on a personality style "state" and "trait" set of items used in psychological profiles employed. Self-reports of interviewers of the "personality style of the individual" were also employed. Those about to retire report they prefer "making plans" compared to "taking action."

The newly retired report themselves less often to be "usually sure and quick in the actions I take." The same group is also least likely to report being "lively individuals." We find those who will retire within a year are most likely to report that they "usually take the initiative in making new friends." They also are more likely to think of themselves as "a lively individual."

When interviewers were asked to rate the respondents' personality, we find those who are newly retired are most likely to be suspicious of the purpose of the study. The display of anger or emotion during the interview with selected topics is reported to be higher by interviewers for those who have recently retired or who are about to retire. Interviewers report those who are about to retire are less likely to be "very" or "somewhat" outgoing.

Overall, we find persons who have been retired for more than a year are not significantly different in their personality styles from those who were not approaching retirement status. On only one item--suspiciousness about the survey--does this group seem to be significantly different. However, what we find is that there are shifts in perceived and self-reported styles. The former group sees themselves as very outgoing in reaching out for social contacts. The latter see themselves more often as better at making plans rather then taking action. Those who have recently retired are more likely to view themselves in a socially withdrawn sense. (See Table XI-3.)

Let us now compare the patterns based on self-reports (Table XI-3) versus those based on reported social contacts (Tables XI-1 and XI-2). We find that the newly retired are reaching out for a variety of informal social contacts but do not see themselves as doing so. There is a discrepancy between the behaviors as reported and self-concept. For those who have been retired for a longer time there is also a discrepancy, but of a different kind. It appears that those retired for longer periods of time see themselves as friendly, outgoing and active. Yet, their informal social ties of neighborhood close friends show a decline. Those retired for more than a year seem to have a personality style that is reaching out for social contact, but the reality of their social experience falls short of this. Persons on the verge of retirement have a high degree of social contact, *and* they see themselves as outgoing. The data we have reviewed hint at a "cognitive dissonance" pattern for persons newly retired and those retired for a longer period. In the case of those just entering the retirement status, they tend to have a self-perception that underestimates the range of social ties they are utilizing. This variance is subsequently altered to one that, in later retirement, consists of a potential for social contact that is not fulfilled in day-to-day reality.

Help Seeking as Community

A major argument in the theoretical exposition contained in Chapter I is that helping networks are a form of social cohesion. If this is true, such social bonds must manifest linkages not just of a helper and a helpee, but the ties between different kinds of helpers. In this definition of a "network," the linkage is indirect: it occurs by the simultaneous seeking of help from one ego to other (A, B, etc.). But "A" and "B" are linked only as a function of an ego's reaching out to both of them. This concept of "organic solidarity" then becomes one manifestation of a "helping community."

What is the evidence that seniors do or do not have "helping communities?" It is not just the use of a person to deal with a problem, but the conjoint use of several helpers. Yet it is more: it is the variety of combinations of helpers, a matrix of ramified helping. How can we measure this notion? In the core study we approached this by utilizing a simple zero-order correlation table. Here, each of the ten kinds of helpers was related to every other helper. Where significant correlations occur we can speak of the "density" or "integrated" character of helping. Without specifically obtaining information on who refers a person to someone else, we can only infer a process of linkages between various helpers. Each contact is, however, a tie involving a specific "behavior area"--that is, the neighborhood, the family, the friendship circle, the workplace, or the community. Helpers need not be the same person, but there are connections between otherwise disparate arenas of primary groups and other social settings and structures. (See Chart XI-1.)

By separating the sample population into those 65 years or older and younger respondents, we can compare the helping networks of the two groups in terms of "integration" among helpers. Of the total of 45 paired correlations among the ten kinds of helpers, we find that persons under age 65 have a statistically significant coefficient (.15 or greater) in a majority of cases--25 times out of 45. By contrast, persons age 65 or older have such links only 15 out of 45 times. (See Appendix Table XI-1.)

Now let us examine the correlated use of specific helper. Clergy shows the widest set of links--five out of a possible 9. Neighbors, friends, and co-workers each have 4 significant links. Doctor, teacher, and police each show 3 links. Despite the general decline in conjoint helper usage for seniors compared to other persons, the neighbor-to-friend overlap is stronger for seniors versus others. The correlations are +.45 and +.56 respectively. The neighbor-to-doctor coefficient is +.45 and for seniors and only +.25 for other persons. The clergy-friend link is +.37 for seniors compared to +.21 for others.

Clearly, neighbors and friends are pivotal helpers for seniors. They are used on a relatively frequent basis and are often linked with the use of other helpers. While co-workers and clergy ties are at the center of several helping links, the low usage of the former by seniors reduces the practical networking of this kind of helper. Clergy are not widely used by either seniors or those under age 65. The differentials between seniors and non-seniors in the "integration" of helping are consistent with many other trends we have noted in other sections of this study. Thus, retirees and seniors are significantly less "organically" tied to society.

Organizational Participation

When we examined the number of voluntary associations that individuals belong to and how this related to seeing their neighbors. (See Chapter VI), we found, that retirees have a mixed pattern of belonging to organizations where they saw neighbors and belonging to others where they did not. In fact, there is very clear evidence of a declining total number of organizations that an individual belongs to once they are retired. But just as the linkage sharply declines once retirement is reached, so we find that the sharpest difference in participation occurs between those on the verge of retirement and those newly retired. Thus, 3.5 organizations is the average for the latter group and 2.0 groups in the former instance. (See TABLE XI-4)

There is some recovery in the number of voluntary organizations belonged to after one has been retired for at least a year, though the level is still below that of the non-retired person. Only two out of five individuals who have been retired more than a year belong to three or more voluntary associations. This contrasts with 52 percent of those not nearing retirement, and 55 percent of those who will retire within a year. Only 8 percent of those who have recently retired belong to at least three voluntary associations. However, 9 out of 10 of those retired for more than a year report belonging to at least one voluntary association. Thus, the isolation from group life of the community is one which is reflected in the multiplicity of organizational memberships rather than in the absence of any ties. (See Table XI-4.)

Church and veterans groups, along with fraternal organizations, are among the types found to represent some of the more frequent examples of retiree memberships. Neighborhood and block club associations also show a high level of participation by retirees. We also find evidence that a significant portion of individuals at various stages in the life cycle report that they are officers or leaders of voluntary associations. Thus, 15 percent of persons retired for more than a year report such a role compared to 21 percent for persons who have not retired. (See Appendix Tables XI-2 and XI-3.)

When sample respondents were asked whether they "know someone who is a leader or an officer in an organization," an affirmative response occurred least among individuals who have been retired for a year or more and most for those who are not nearing retirement status. The differential is 20 versus 33 percent respectively. Putting together the actual leadership role and knowledge about others who are in such a role, we see that what is characteristic of retirement status is a withdrawal from linkages to those in leadership roles rather than memberships per se.

Individuals may still serve in a leadership role, but lack ties to others who are in the same position. Such a pattern is more common for those retired for at least one year. They belong to few organizations and tend to lack knowledge about key leaders in groups. They are not part of a network of organizational activists as often as other people. That is to say, the "organic integration" of the retired person is more likely to be interrupted than the "mechanical solidarity." (See Table XI-5.)

Sources of Information: Media versus Personal Contact

Retirement and the constriction of social involvement can be manifested in a variety of ways. Ties of primary and secondary group participation are clearly central. We have seen evidence of the decline in both of these arenas of human interaction. The declining face-to face contacts, both in organizations and in primary groups, might well suggest that the whole of the electronic and print media may be able to provide an alternative or compensatory mechanism for the social integration of retirees.

One of the questions that was asked in the survey dealt with the use of various sources of information in "getting hints or ideas on how to deal with the things that we have been talking about." Here we are referring to the list of "recent concerns." The twelve different sources of information were provided in a list to indicate whether these were "very" or "somewhat" or "not at all important." Not surprisingly, for a variety of groups in the survey, the electronic media were highly significant. Thus, for those individuals who were newly retired, television commentators and special TV programs are mentioned to a significantly higher degree than for those who were nearing retirement. This is also the case for radio, with the newly retired using this resource to a greater extent than any group in the analysis. Seventy-seven percent of this group reported using radio for hints or ideas compared to 60 percent for those who have been retired for more than a year, 56 percent for those on the verge of retirement, and 49 percent of those not nearing retirement age. The same group also reported using newspapers, magazines and opinion polls to a significantly greater degree than any other group in the survey.

The newly retired seem to seek information from all sources and to they had the highest average amount of information seeking in terms of the rate of importance of various media sources. Those on the verge of retirement show a smaller range of resources being used. (See Appendix Table XI-4.)

For the total sample, electronic media comprise 62 percent of the reported sources of helpful information. What distinguishes those who have been retired for more than a year from other groups is their decline in the use of primary group information sources. Those who have very recently retired rely significantly less on electronic media and more on personal influence sources. (See TABLE XI-6)

By turning to the electronic media, with the subsequent decline of primary groups ties, persons retired for longer than a year may be linked to the larger society in ways that are less personal yet less isolated than the newly retired. Another way to approach this is to look at the responses to the open-ended questions about "the kinds of problems that people in this community face" in terms of the "size" of (local, non-local) of the sphere of involvement of those problems. We find that those who are newly retired are more likely to define a problem in terms of the neighborhood context. They are least likely to focus on their surrounding community. Persons who are not nearing retirement status are the least likely to speak about problems in terms of the neighborhood sphere. There is no significant difference between retirees and others in terms of problems which emphasize a national level.

The patterns shown in Table XI-7 underscore the sense in which the newly retired may indeed shrink their world to the neighborhood and show, that, after a period there is a rebounding or expansion into the spheres of integration that go beyond the immediate locality. Regarding the use of media by those retired for more than a year, results are consistent with a view that this group is attending to events and activities beyond the neighborhood. (See TABLE XI-7)

Political Participation of Seniors

One of the more general measures of social integration with the large society is political participation. The Gray Panther movement of the 1960's as well as the Townsend Movement of the 1930's offers abundant evidence that seniors can become a political force. Smith and Turk (1966) discuss the role of age in community integration. On the question of the integrative situation of the aged in the community, the authors suggest two concerns: first, whether the older person has more or less the same amount of "integrative attributes" as other population segments. For example, the authors, in raising the question of whether voting rates compare with other adults, pose the following hypotheses:

> Given a mechanism that may have integrative consequences for the urban community, the data suggest that the more accessible, the more public, the more individualistic, the less subtle and sophisticated, and the more unselectively ascriptive its organization, the greater the likelihood that an older population will compare favorably with a younger one (Smith and Turk, p. 252).

Anaylst by James Trela, suggests that:

> The high voting levels of the aged population, their tendency to give rather than to receive political orientation, and their high levels of interest in political activity on the media suggests that the aged are intensely interested in and committed to political processes. That their age compels older individuals to act alike politically is less certain however.

There is evidence in the present study that those who are retired are politically active and this is directly expressed by two questions dealing with voting behavior. Eighty-six percent of those retired for more than a year reported that they voted in the presidential election of 1972. Seventy-seven percent of the same group reported having voted in the gubernatorial election of November 1974. Voting behavior of those nearing or beyond the initial retirement status show a higher level of voting than persons retired within one year. (See Table XI-8.)

Is there a linkage between the neighborhood and that wider world? We used several measures of perceived and actual social contact and helping in the neighborhood and correlated this with voting in the 1972 presidential election. For persons that are 65 years or older, there were significant positive linkages between the perception of neighborhoods, of belonging to outside groups, of getting together in the neighborhood and of having things in common, as well as the frequency of actually visiting with neighbors.

Voting is also positively correlated with having a unit of neighborhood larger than the local block. Thus, 93 percent of seniors who say their neighborhood is "walking distance" report voting in the presidential election of 1972. Of particular interest is the positive correlation between the number of helpers used in coping with recent concerns and voting. Moreover, contact with friends and relatives does not have the positive affect on voting that was found for the various neighborhood indicators. (See Table XI-9.)

Following Up on the Survey: Some Participation Indicators

As part of the original study, a series of questions was asked in the follow-up interviews a year later. Those concerned the ways in which people might want to participate in feed-back about the results of the study and possibly aid in the stimulation of helping processes among neighbors. In regard to wanting to receive additional reports on findings of the study, there is a lower level of interest expressed by those retired for more than a year, with the highest level of interest expressed by those who will retire within a year. On a more specifically participatory question, that is, would people "go to a meeting in the neighborhood to discuss the problems talked about in the interview," 50 percent of those retired for more than a year indicated that they would do so. This compares with only 40 percent for those newly retired. Those on the verge of retirement showed the highest level of interest in this kind of meeting: 70 percent. (See TABLE XI-9)

In regard to joining a group dealing with "the things discussed in the interviews," the highest level is found for those who are nearing retirement-- 39 percent. The lowest level was among those who have been retired for more than a year--21 percent. Respondents were also asked: "Would you be willing to host a meeting in your own home of a small group to discuss the problems talked about in the survey?" Here we find that those newly retired are least likely to indicate willingness to do so--only 6 percent. More than twice as many of those persons retired for more than a year indicate such a willingness to host a meeting. The highest levels are found for the persons approaching retirement and those who are in other positions.

The data shown in Table XI-10 provide evidence that is not consistent with a view that a neighborhood or general social mobilization declines steadily once retirement status is reached. Willingness and interest *vis a vis* the various suggested survey follow-up actions is lowest for those newly retired. However, in two out of four instances a rebound occurs for those retired for a year or more. This does not reach the level of very high response to the participation question that is manifested by those about to retire. (See Table XI-10.)

Summary

There are several suggestions from the data discussed in this chapter indicating that significant changes take place in the social integration of those who retire. Primary group ties are less frequently renewed by visiting and the size of such networks appear to shrink. But the increase in what might be termed "social isolation" has several facets: reduced personal influence, contact, and restricted indirect network linkages. This latter point means that aging members of urban communities do not have ramified ties via helping and organizational participation. They are less often in touch with a wider sphere of friends of friends, friends of neighbors, leaders in organizations and social arenas that are not directly tapped by face-to-face contact. This reduction in "organic" social integration has been a less visible aspect of the more dramatic "mechanical" isolation that many seniors experience.

Ties to the wider community and nation dip immediately after retirement, but appear to rebound again. Moreover, a strong link to the local neighborhood through perceptions about its cohesiveness and strength play a role in voting behavior. There is a kind of platform of social assurance that occurs by neighborhood serving as the base for participation in the larger society. For those immediately coping with retirement, neighborhood appears to be more of a self-contained and exclusive sphere of involvement. This appears to give way--at least potentially--to the role of an integration of neighborhood with the larger community.

Specific opportunities for social participation at either the neighborhood level or via the electronic media may be instrumental avenues for involving the retired and aging in ways that their previous intimate networks of social support may sometimes be unable to do. The technology of communication has not been applied to the neighborhood level and particularly to the interest of seniors or retirees in making contact beyond their local area. This social policy agenda is hinted at in the data we have reviewed in this chapter.

TABLE XI-1

Frequent versus No Visiting Contact with Relatives Friends, and Neighbors

	Retired more than 1 year before interview	Retired within the last year	To retire within 1 year after interview	Other persons inter-viewed
	Visit at least once a week			
Kin	46%	59%	49%	47%
Friends	26%	32%	33%	33%
Neighbors	18%	19%	18%	20%
	Never visit			
Kin	4%	2%	0%	2%
Friends	9%	9%	5%	4%
Neighbors	36%	26%	38%	29%
TOTAL:				
Frequent vs.	90%	110%	100%	100%
never	49%	37%	43%	35%
Difference	+41%	+73%	+57%	+65%
Ratio:	1.8:1	3.0:1	2.3:1	2.9:1

TABLE XI-2

Size of Informal Social Networks

	Retired more than 1 year before interview	Retired within the last year	To retire within 1 year after interview	Other persons inter-viewed
Number of relatives who are close friends	11.8	11.4	15.6+	10.2
Number of close friends living in the metropolitan area	16.6	29.7+	19.7	16.2
Number of close friends who live outside of metropolitan area	11.1−	15.3−	19.6	18.3
Neighbors who are close friends	5.0	3.3−	8.4+	4.2
Close friends at work	0.5	1.1	8.0	6.1
Overall average	9.0−	12.2	14.3+	11.0

TABLE XI-3

Personality Style of the Respondent: Self-Descriptions and Interviewer Impressions

	Retired more than 1 year before interview	Retired within the last year	To retire within 1 year after interview	Other persons inter-viewed
	Percent Saying "True"			
"I prefer action to making plans"	57%	44%–	45%–	57%
"I am usually sure and quick in my actions"	61%	38%–	65%	62%
"I usually take the initiative in making new friends	64%	69%	82%+	66%
"I would be unhappy if I weren't around a lot of people	44%	44%	40%	45%
"I think of myself as a lively individual"	73%	63%–	80%+	74%
Interviewer reports R is very or some-what outgoing	74%	69%–	68%–	79%
Respondent got excited, angry, emotional or displayed hostility for parts of interview	10%	20%+	22%+	9%
Respondent was very suspicious about the study before the interview	16%	25%+	13%	8%–

TABLE XI-4

Number of Organizations Respondent Belongs To

	Retired more than 1 year before interview	Retired within the last year	To retire within 1 year after interview	Other persons inter-viewed
None	9%	9%	5%	8%
One	25	36+	15	19
Two	26	28	25	21
Three	18	11	18	19
Four	12	8	15	12
Five or more	10	8	22+	21+
TOTAL	100%	100%	100%	100%
Mean	2.4	2.0	3.5	3.0

TABLE XI-5

Number of Organizations Respondent Belongs To

	Retired more than 1 year before interview	Retired within the last year	To retire within 1 year after interview	Other persons inter-viewed
None	9%	9%	5%	8%
One	25	36+	15	19
Two	26	28	25	21
Three	18	11	18	19
Four	12	8	15	12
Five or more	10	8	22+	21+
TOTAL	100%	100%	100%	100%
Mean	2.4	2.0	3.5	3.0

TABLE XI-6

Information Sources for "Problems Like the Ones we Have Discussed" in Terms of Media and Personal Influence

		Retired more than 1 year before interview	Retired within the last year	To retire within 1 year after interview	Other persons inter-viewed
Media	Electronic	33%[*] +	27%	29%	29%
		62% {	55% {	54% {	58% {
	Written	29	28	25	29
Personal influence	Primary group	29 –	32	35	33
	Secondary group	9	13	11	9
Total		100%	100%	100%	100%

*Percentages are based on adding all percentages of "very" or "somewhat" important for each of the 13 indicated information sources and then dividing that total in terms of which fall into the above four categories. The values obtained are thus percentages of the sum of individual percentages.

TABLE XI-7

Sphere of Involvement for General Problems

	Retired more than 1 year before interview	Retired within the last year	To retire within 1 year after interview	Other persons inter-viewed
Problem involves neighborhood of respondent	30%	43%+	26%	17%−
Problem involves community (city) in which R lives	38	23−	41	45
Problem involves the nation (beyond the city)	31	33	32	36
Problem involves the world (beyond U.S.)	1	0	0	1
Total	100%	99%	99%	99%

TABLE XI-8

Voting Behavior of Persons in the
Four Analysis Groups

	Retired more than 1 year before interview	Retired within the last year	To retire within 1 year after interview	Other persons inter-viewed
		Percent Yes		
"Many people were not able to vote in the last presidential election. Did you vote in the Presidential election in 1972?	86%	81%	85%	78%
"What about the last election for governor in November 1974. Did you vote in that election?"	77%	75%	80%	71%

TABLE XI-9

Voting in the 1972 Presidential Election for Persons
65 or older in Relation to
Selected Social Integration

Perception that
neighbors belong
to outside groups $\qquad$ $g = +.39^*$

Perception that
people in the
neighborhood get
together for visits $\qquad$ $g = +.33^*$

Perception that
people in the
neighborhood have
things in common $\qquad$ $g = +.20^*$

Perceived
neighborhood area
is large $\qquad$ $g = .+17^*$

Sum of differend kinds
of helpers used for
recent concerns $\qquad$ $g = +.16^*$

Frequency of visiting
friends $\qquad$ $g = +.00$

Like neighborhood $\qquad$ $g = -.08$

Frequent visits with
relatives $\qquad$ $g = -.09$

TABLE XI-10

**Participation as a Follow-up to the Helping Network
Study**

	Retired more than 1 year before interview	Retired within the last year	To retire within 1 year after interview	Other persons inter-viewed
	Percent saying "Yes"			
"Would you like to receive additional reports on the findings of our study?"	67% –	81%	90% +	81%
"If there were a meeting in your neighbohood about the problems we've talked about in this interview, would you be interested in attending?"	50%	40%	70% +	63%
"Would you be interested in joining a group dealing with the things talked about in the interview?"	21%	25%	39% +	29%
"Would you be willing to host a small group in your home for one or more meetings?"	13% –	6% –	25% +	20%

chart XI-1

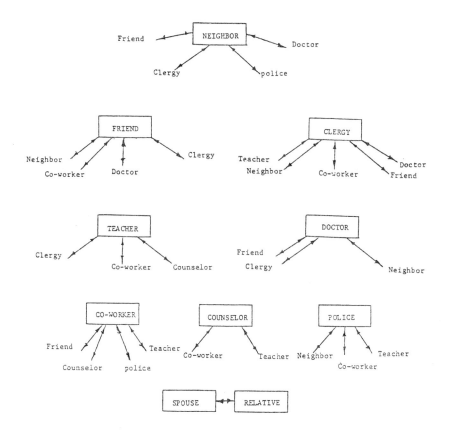

Helping Linkages for Each Type of Helper

CHAPTER XII

SUMMARY DISCUSSION: IMPLICATIONS FOR THEORY
AND SOME PROGRAMMATIC THEMES

As we noted in the introductory commentary, much of the conceptual framework utilized in this presentation derives from *post hoc* theory. This particular application of the helping network study to seniors and retirees was generated by a good deal of rethinking of the original empirical findings. This point is particularly salient in approaching the effort in this chapter to draw together the various results and to restate the major themes that we have treated. For it is certainly the case that much of the focus on the aging and retired must be considered exploratory rather than definitive in character.

Summary of Key findings: Results of a Multivariate Analysis

Let us first review the results derived from a comprehensive examination of all of the major variables employed in the analysis. To accomplish this, we have utilized a statistical methodology that has been developed to discover the "structure" of a set of independent predictors on a given dependent variable. That outcome measure we have labeled "risk to well being." It is utilized as a general variable in assessment of the quality of life of the sample population. By use of the A.I.D. program (Automatic Interaction Detection), developed at the University of Michigan, we can survey all of the social attachment and demographic variables that may affect the life of seniors as well as others in the helping-network study. This technique of multivariate analysis is a form of step-wise regression which produces a splitting of the sample into groups that score "high" or "low" on the dependent variable--in this case the RISK score. The central questions that can be addressed with this method are: 1) How much total variance can be explained by the additive effects of independent variables? and 2) What amount of interaction between these variables is also present?

When the A.I.D. statistical program is carried out for two separate subgroups of the helping network sample--those 65 or older and those under age 65--a number of different relationships emerge in terms of the values on the RISK indicator as a dependent variable. Of major importance is the fact that much more of the total variance can be explained for seniors using a set of primary group, secondary group and neighborhood predictors than is the case for non-seniors. Essentially what occurs is that 22.7 percent of the total variance in RISK score can be explained by using 11 neighborhood related variables, 7 non-neighborhood social tie variables, and 6 demographic attributes of the respondent along with a measure of concern about energy related shortages. By contrast, these same 26 variables explain only 13.7 percent of the variance in the RISK score for non-seniors. (See TABLE XII-1)

Using the Beta weight values derived from the A.I.D. analysis--which are equivalent to measures of the strength of a given variable taking out the effect of other correlated variables--results in a far larger contribution to the total explained variance for seniors in terms of both the neighborhood and non-neighborhood social tie variables. Demographic variables of race, income, marital status, age, and employment status as well as education are also important sources of explained variance in RISK score for both seniors and non-seniors.

One of the features of the A.I.D. program is that it selects the most powerful predictor variables and then divides the sample into a "high" and a "low" group in terms of the dependent variable--in this case the RISK score. The result is the structuring of a "tree" of split groups as the search for explained variance further divides the sample on important independent variable categories. The first of these "trees" is shown in Chart XII-1. We note in the beginning the most powerful way to split the sample of seniors is on the basis of the interviewer's judgement about the physical condition and quality of public facilities in the immediate neighborhood where the respondent lives. Following this initial division, the six-fold neighborhood typology then emerges and is in fact the most powerful of the neighborhood-related variables in terms of Beta weight values. Amount of neighbor visiting and several indicators of kin and friend contacts also emerge as powerful variables in the effects that alter the RISK score of seniors.

Not only do the selected predictor variables explain less of the total variance in RISK score of non-seniors, but the particular form of the A.I.D. tree is sharply different from that of seniors. (See Table XII-1.) The first or most powerful split comes not on a neighborhood variable for non-seniors but on reported family income. Moreover, demographic variables play a relatively more important role for non-seniors in comparison to seniors. At the same time the role of community emerges as a more significant predictor of RISK score for non-seniors compared to seniors. (See CHARTS XII-1 & 2)

The Role of Problems and the Unique Function of "Recent Concerns"

The multivariate analysis of RISK clarifies the disparate findings in regard to the nexus of social contact and neighborhood variables in shaping the quality of life of seniors. At the same time, we should note a major source of RISK that was indicated in Chapter III: that of "problem load." The RISK score was high correlated with the number of "recent concerns." As was noted in the report of the general helping network findings (Warren, 1976, 1979) such worries and desires to changes one's life appear to be more powerful sources of the behaviors described in the RISK measure than are the selected Holmes and Rahe items that we have defined as "life crises."

While persons age 65 or older and those who are retired have a generally low "recent concern" load compared to others, these items do powerfully affect well-being for these groups. We found substantial evidence in Chapters IV and V that who helps, the number of helpers, and the type of help provided for these concerns importantly determines the level of RISK that accompanies their occurance. Particularly as the help is diversified in kind and range of helpers is it liable to reduce the apparent stress-accompanying "recent concern." These findings therefore underscore the paradox of help seeking as a healthy process that is often provoked by negative elements in the social environment of both the aging and the general population.

Our analysis suggests that "recent concerns" are "non-uniform" tasks related to the concepted employed by Litwak (1983). They are not only tasks or problems that are "low" in "invoked expertise" because no specialized bureaucracy or professional problem-coping system has been instituted or claims jurisdiction over their solution; but they also are not directly linked to a set of behaviors specific to their handling. Thus, "life crises" of the Holmes and Rahe variety involved a severing of a close social tie or the handling of an emergency situation. As such, one can anticipate the need for particular kinds of behaviors such as sympathetic listening or immediate transportation of the person injured or ill. But in the case of "recent concerns," a similar range of helping behaviors to that used for crises may be employed--it is not at all clear what particular one or combination of several is most valued, effective, or significant in problem coping.

It is possible to consider that the only criterion of a satisfactory helping relationship is the congruence between what people want and what they receive in the way of help. For purposes of the present study, that is virtually the only model we can employ. How well does it apply to "non-uniform" "recent concerns"? First of all, since there is no standard to judge what is useful, we can only consider what people say they want. If they receive this form of help, then in some intrinsic way the helping is "appropriate" and therefore "effective" in some sense. A concept of reciprocity may also apply: people seek the help that they may be most able to give themselves.

Given the nature of "recent concerns," they are seldom placed in the hands of formal agencies orprofessionals, and which are highly ideosyncratic in their solution. We argue that their effects on well-being must be measured more subjectively by the formula of "balance" between help wanted, help obtained, and help given when one is asked in turn to be a helper and not a help seeker.

Recent concerns are a special variety of "non-uniform" task in that they are not only problems which require autonomy, internalization, and non-standardized behaviors in their solution, but also that the *variety* of such non-uniform elements suggests totally different needs or strategies of problem coping. Is it best to "show a person a new way to look at the problem" of retirement or to "just listening"? What is the best way to deal with simple depression? Each of several answers--whether it be sympathetic listening, asking questions, or even taking action--involves rather distinct and inconsistent directions of problem helping. Diverse combinations can further elaborate the range of approaches.

It is very doubtful that even placing the task in the hands of a "human relations" trained professional could resolve the diversity of reasonable approaches that might be taken. Given this unique variability, there is clearly no way that criteria of effectiveness might emerge apart from the reports of the helpee or their return to the same helper might suggest.

The Diverse Nature of Urban Social Ties: A Symbiotic Pattern

Urban social ties can be dichotomized into bases of "mechanical" and "organic" solidarity[9]. Those involving direct (mechanical) social bonds include: 1) traditional primary groups, 2) task groups such as in a work setting or voluntary organization and 3) close-knit social networks. Each shares small size, intimacy of relationships, and common values of the individuals involved. There are three forms of "organic" solidarity: 1) problem-anchored helping networks, 2) loose-knit social networks, and 3) weak ties. Each of these has in common the lack of dependence of face-to-face communication, infrequent interaction, specialized spheres of "expertise" or "jurisdiction" (or problem-solving capacity), and diverse social composition.

The essential argument is that a mixture of both types of social patterns--mechanically and organically based--provide the most effective and salutary forms of community life in a contemporary society. The nature of human community is problem coping--particularly as it is organized in terms of organic solidarity. Neither social networks nor primary groups provide the basis of organic community. Each is a necessary but not sufficient component of organic community. "Loose-knit" ties are not usually effective for utilitarian goals. Having both kinds of group ties is an optimal pattern for the individual and also insures the well-being of a community through the "balance" of tight and loose-knit ties (see Warren Dunham, 1977).

The Bridging Roles of Problem-Anchored Helping Networks

A wide variety of social ties may exist in the behavior settings of the neighborhood, the workplace and the voluntary association. It is possible to characterize the mix of forms for a whole community or population or for a given individual within a specific locale. We have posited a functional balance theory of loose- and tight-knit ties. Loose-knit ties are largely problem centered and seldom serve as bases for expressive needs. A pivotal role in the linkage between these varieties of informal social ties is played by problem-anchored helping networks: they overlap both traditional close-knit and the dispersed, loose-knit patterns of a given population group or individual.

There are at least three major ways in which problem-anchored helping networks act in a bridging or brokerage role between an individual's loose- and tight-knit ties by creating or strengthening one or the other type. First, there is the fact of keeping alive (as a loose tie) some aspect of a relationship with former members of close-knit social groups. Rather than geographic movement or social mobility totally severing contact with a former work group, neighborhood, or organization, occasional help seeking can maintain knowledge about the activities and whereabouts of former intimates. Even though none of the present members of a problem-anchored network may have been part of that earlier close-knit group, there is a greater-than-random chance probability of a present neighbor knowing a former neighbor, a present workmate knowing a prior one, or the people now active in a local chapter of a civic organization knowing a former member. All of these links enhance the opportunity of present social contact with those who are no longer one's intimates.

Secondly, problem anchored helping networks serve as potential spawning grounds for the creation of new close-knit ties by virtue of the shared problems and "crises" that occasionally emerge. These infrequent events intensify the social ties that are otherwise relatively specific in focus and bring together members of the network so that they each come to know each other. Such instances may range from the severe winter (not just a bad snow storm) that requires neighbors to help each other in large numbers or over a longer "problem" sequence than is the case for such helping as watching a home when a neighbor is on vacation or keeping an eye on children playing in the street.

A threat of school bussing, urban renewal clearance, or traffic hazards may bring neighbors together in ways that were previously lacking in collective dimensions and enduring social action. These potential problem incidents can be found in the work setting and the voluntary association context as well. Such events are idiosyncratic and are not the normal basis of helping. Moreover, they generally do not spillover into linkages with other groups or individuals. But individuals rooted in a single setting may begin to call upon helpers outside of that milieu and to therefore mobilize a network of helping ties which may bring together individuals in a face-to-face and intimate sense as a "social web" who were previously linked solely by their having been referrals from one person in a proximity-based social setting.

The third way in which problem-anchored social networks bridge or strengthen other social ties is by creating a base of reciprocity in terms of past favors or help. While there are no requirements for such reciprocity they are relationships in which "the norm of reciprocity" is implied even if it is not immediately satisfied. It is this future contingency of a social tie that provides continuity to "loose-knit" relationships and may require the "cashing in" of favors precisely in one of the problems or crisis situations where close-knit ties are likely to be built.

Functional Specialization and the Diverse Capacities of Neighborhoods

Litwak and his colleagues point out that the structure of the neighborhood provides a different context for reciprocity than does the kin group:

> Neighbors like 'acquaintances' may be reluctant to accept large amounts of help from each other or to offer it and be anxious to return favors as soon as possible, owing to the short-term,

somewhat transitory nature of the relationship (Dono, Litwak, *et al.*, 1978, p.4).

By contrast, researchers such as Cantor find "the nature of supportive exchanges occurring between the elderly and their neighbors...are often behaviorly reflective of a blurring of the distinction between friends and neighbors." Yet in her empirical data Cantor also finds a split between help and social interaction:

> Knowing one or more neighbors well...may not in and of itself insure a helping relationship of an exchange nature exists between elderly and the neighbor. In fact, applying the more stringent criterion of functionality--not only well but evidence of interaction--indicates 9 percent of respondents knowing a neighbor well are not in a function social support relationship with such neighbors (Cantor, 1977, pg. 12).

These findings, as well as the analysis by Litwak and his colleagues, can be integrated under the conceptual framework we have exposited in the current study. To call upon a neighbor is less an act of affirmation of "sense of community" than it is a testing of "what is out there." Our data shows that seniors and retirees, regardless of their "objective" neighborhood, are quite often testing out the extent of resources of help and social support that neighbors can provide. What occurs once that system has been tried out differs markedly from one type of neighborhood to another. It would indeed be clear that by making sure of the limited resources and finding that the help is appropriate will intensify the probability of further help.

It would indeed be valid to conclude that no objective reality of neighborhood can fully describe the "idea of neighborhood" that people may carry in their heads. Thus, the neighbor can be a referral agent, and, at the same time, can provide instrumental help on a range of problems that are not strictly neighborhood problems. To the extent that such a pattern may occur, we would argue that it is not dependent on the skills of the help seeker, although one shall not rule out the selective search that may go on but it is a question of what is potentially out there in the neighborhood. But at the same time our earlier findings have underscored the fact that if the help seeker, particularly the senior, perceives the neighborhood to have a potential of helping resources, they will then carry their search out more extensively than they otherwise would.

Cantor points out that the nature of problem specialization is such that the distinction between "instrumental" help and "social support" is likely to reflect itself in how neighbor help occurs. One of our major findings is that the senior or retired person is likely to seek help from neighbors in a less specialized fashion and, therefore, to seek out help for problems of loneliness as well as with someone to help with a leaking faucet.

There is little question about the fact that use of neighbor help is often not a product of positive social attraction, but of simple necessity. That is to say, many problems in which help is used involve negative conditions of the neighborhood. We did not find that neighborhood problems were the ones for which retired and aging residents turned to neighbors. Thus, we cannot support the view that use of neighbor help for these particular social groups is especially mainly in response to emergency or crisis needs for accessible help.

We do find some evidence of functional substitution occuring in regard to neighbor help for new problems and a range of non-neighborhood problems. This substitution is not due to the intrinsic fact that the task-specific elements of the problem reflect the particular skills of neighboring. Rather we find the decline in accessibility of other helpers, such as kin or friends, is linked to the fact of a *neighborhood having a social fabric that is supportive*--of a bridge to other help.

Our study indicates that neighborhood is not so much an alternative to formal agency helping or a link to kin and "significant others" as it is an arena within which the individual is integrated or isolated from a larger world of helping resources, information, and social support. Neighborhood is not so much a *place* where social closeness flourishes as it is a "potential" community whose resources may be hidden from the view of a given individual by barriers of personal time investment, social distance or the degree to which an individual is experiencing a particular kind of problem.

Some Principles of Program Design

The research undertaken in this study of seniors and retirees is too general in nature to provide the basis for specific social program design to specific social program designs to strengthen the helping networks of seniors.

But there seems to be several basic concepts that are supported by the data we have reported upon. We may call these "policy principles" or propositions that need to be taken into account in the design of various programs to aid the quality of life of seniors and retirees. We will now indicate these as follows:

1. The principle that the neighborhood should not be treated as a self-contained community.

2. The principle of reciprocity--help given and help received.

3. The need to bridge helping roles between over-specialized instrumental versus social support types of aid.

4. The relative nature of functional substitutibility in friend, neighbor and kin helping.

5. The development of options based on "loose-knit" and "tight-knit" ties of neighborhoods and helping networks.

Neighborhood as a Gateway

On the first point, we must stress once again the fact that seniors appear to use the neighborhood as a building block not as a retreat in its best form. Therefore, the goal of neighborhood-based programs to the elderly should not be to increase the self-contained role of service and resources, but to build a capacity for ties beyond the neighborhood. As we have commented upon in Chapter XI there is a great deal of evidence to support the view that seniors withdraw from many face-to-face contacts and turn to electronic and mass media sources of information. The discussion by Black and Bengston (1977) suggests that new forms of two-way television technology, as well as similar two-way cable telecommunications may be a particular resource for seniors and retirees. They argue that these emerging technological innovations may be particularly valuable to seniors in terms of putting them in touch with service agencies from their homes.

With cable telecommunications, a widow will use her television directory to find the right process to go through and will fill out all the forms sitting in her living room. The computer will be able to verify the various records involved.

> You're still sitting in your living room where you can fill out all the forms by answering the TV screen, and the computer leads you to whatever information is needed to complete them. The computer can probably verify your marriage and death record.

The authors go on to say

> although such innovations will benefit everyone, they will perhaps be of greatest help to the elderly....Political activity appears to be a frequent victim of social disengagement...a community information system might help to maintain political activity, if such a system could somehow mitigate involuntary losses of social support. Such a system could perhaps be designed to allow the individual to identify and interact with people of similar interests, thus increasing the probability of a restoration of some kind of meaningful social connectiveness following a social loss (Black and Bengston, 1977, p. 274).

The discussion of communications linkages of the type suggested by Black and Bengston is consistent with findings on information sources noted in Chapter XI. A wide variety of efforts to create "skill banks" in neighborhoods and the experiments with two-way television communications offer creative possibilities.

Reciprocity

In regard to the principle of reciprocity, we have already indicated the goal of programs for the elderly and retired should be to examine very carefully ways in which the role of the helper, no matter how oriented toward a human relations approach, may still provide for only one-way communication. In the absence of a mutuality of information and expertise exchanged, the success of such linkages may indeed be limited and may prove to be contrary or dysfunctional to their original goals.

One of the reasons that the senior may strongly emphasize what Cantor and Mayer call the "fiercely independent" nature of inner-city aging in their response to hypothetical service-need situations is that they are unable to engage in reciprocated help giving. If it is true that, for example, instrumental help is given, such as someone coming over to help in an illness, or to take someone shopping or to provide a specific contact with an agency or organization, and then the helpee is unable to provide, in turn, their own form of instrumental "grass roots expertise, then we see another reason why such reaching out may cause one to be uncomfortable when one does engage in help seeking.

The concept of reciprocity helping implies a status-equal role. We are all aware of the fact that formal agencies are engaging in a series of strategies to reduce the social distance between clients and professional staff. It is clear that, in regard to the position of seniors and retirees, the absence of normatively defined workloads and formal educational linguistic and technical bases of common interest further erode the sense of shared status between helper and helpee. It is clearly the case that the stress inherent in service delivery strategies for the aged is on the "informal support system" must require then not only the narrowing of social distance and the dividing of helping strategy that sets aside status-educational and life-experience differential, but must also provide an opportunity for the true exchange of information and expertise between "client and professional."

Lack of reciprocal helping may explain why programs which are specifically targeted to the elderly will fail in their goals of maximizing service delivery for reasons quite apart from the technical skill and even the style of service and delivery. Such programs may simply generate a set of needs to reciprocate when, in fact, the senior may be unable to do so. This may be a major reason to explain the withdrawal of seniors from such relationships.

Reciprocity is even more critical when we see the whole style of program delivery aimed at the elderly which seeks to so debureaucratize and deformalize service delivery that it sets up expectations about status equality and reciprocity which may in fact not be fulfilled This may generate a sense of perceived inconsistency even on the part of the service giver in regard to the true nature of their program. Thus, wherever the expectation of status-equal mutual aid or "informal helping" is generated, the requirements on the service agency to live up to this expectation becomes far more difficult to implement than might be the case where the population being served has reason to see itself deferring to the expertise of the agency.

The potential for alienation from service deliverers who present themselves as informal support networks may become great among seniors and retirees. Seniors may be more willing to accept and trust the formal specialized expert if they have an expectation that this is the kind of help that they finally need. Thus, one should be very cautious about shifting the nature of programming for the elderly to an informal social-support network when, in fact, that may not be the only type of help the senior is seeking and, in particular, when the reality of the helping relationship cannot fulfill a reciprocated helping role. As Don Schon remarks:

> Informal social networks would seem to be an indispensible component of any program to which government attempts to foster independence and self-reliance among those who are perceived to be in some way handicapped. Informal networks are essential to the success of any intervention with the espoused objective of "cattlizing change," encouraging the diffusion of practices and techniques, or facilitating social learning....Indeed, the rhetoric of governmental policy in fields such as education, corrections, human services, rehabilitation, health--the field known as social policy--seems to point inexorably in the direction of interventions which take informal social networks into account (Schon, 1977, p. 60).

Overcoming Program Specialization

The concept of bridging specialized kinds of helping roles is one that has been commented upon by several researchers and in which data in the present study suggest a need to examine whether the program of a given group can in fact "piggy-back" on to the goals of a group with far different specialization.

One of the most popular programs for dealing with services to the elderly involves the concept of formulating a block level of organization. The positive side of this is that such a program permits a network to be established which covers an entire geographic area. At the same time, as was found in the case of the senior block information service (SBIS) this program seemed to work most effectively precisely where there was a great deal of flexibility in what the active volunteer did in carrying out this program. As this program evolved, however, it took on more of the characteristics of a specialized bureaucratic effort. Its original goal of building self-help was replaced by the creation of a quasi-bureaucratic structure of volunteers and professional helpers who distribute newsletters and provide information to seniors. Therefore, the original goal of building communities via such a program does not seem to have emerged. But at the same time a new infrastructure of information and contact has been established. (See Ruffini, Todd *et al.*, 1979 and Ruffini and Todd, 1979).

Programs for the elderly dealing with housing maintenance offer another example of the tendency toward too great a functional specialization in helping the "target" population. Such housing "fix-up" efforts have been developed in a number of urban centers. There is a general pattern of identifying a technical "uniform" task without also exploring other needs as well while the home visit is being conducted. Examples have included assistance to people for insulating and improving the condition of their home that, at the same time, is linked to social agencies. The individual who is trained to go out to accomplish a technical task such as trying to determine the need for weather stripping or fixing a door lock also be trained as a good listener and as someone who may pick up the social and emotional problems that seniors and retirees may be experiencing. Such understanding and bridges between task and social-emotional roles of helpers can be accomplished in a variety of contexts including all of the programs that are operated by agencies such as human service and police organizations.

The intuitively wise helper, of course, does bridge such a gap. Often, the most successful social programs have naturally evolved a flexibility in responding across these kinds of functional task distinctions. But we are suggesting that special attention be paid to generating this range of capacities in any local social network program.

Functional Substitution in Program Design

The nature of neighborhood may be such that it may turn in the direction of functions often provided by kin or in the directions often provided by casual acquaintances. It is precisely in this diffuse character of the neighborhood that we may see a breakdown in problem specialization that occurs for individuals that are tied to the neighborhood in the more specialized ways that are reflective of persons at a stage of life prior to retirement and advanced age. Because of the structural complexity of the neighborhood, therefore, we would argue that the neighborhood may indeed become a functional substitute for other informal or primary group helping systems. We stress very strongly that this is not generally going to be the case for neighborhoods.

Variability of Neighborhood Fabric

Human service providers must identify salient dimensions of local community social fabric in order to reach sound judgements about whether a given neighborhood may perform a multi-functional or a single specialized functional role in the life of seniors and retirees. A neighborhood may even develop the social form of a formal bureaucracy. It may have highly specialized roles and a complex hierarchy of leadership and of intermediate and quasi-formal helping. There may be reputational activists in the neighborhood to which an individual may turn rather than simply to a next-door neighbor. There may be heads of local organizations that are seen as highly expert on the problem of what to do in organizing the neighborhood in the event of some threat to it such as a polluting industry or a nuisance enterprise.

A Closing Note

The analysis of the helping networks of seniors and retirees has provided an opportunity to consider a number of issues that relate to basic dimensions of the quality of life of this growing segment of our society. In approaching these problems we have utilized a small sample drawn from a comprehensive survey of several divergent communities and neighborhoods.

Many of the key findings we have reported on, represent only working hypotheses that might be refined and tested far more rigorously than was possible within the framework of this secondary analysis design. In particular, caution must be exercised in the conclusions drawn about early versus later retirement. We were able to compare a small number of people who became retirees and then see if their social patterns reflected this change of status.

Continued testing and evaluating the findings of this study can be carried out in future research by the use of such techniques as continuous diary information and repeated sampling of people as they move through several stages of pre-and post-retirement life. All of these approaches will be helpful in revising or re-affirming key concepts and conclusions we have presented.

CHART XII-1

Automatic Interaction Detection (A.I.D.) Analysis

For Respondents Age 65 or Older

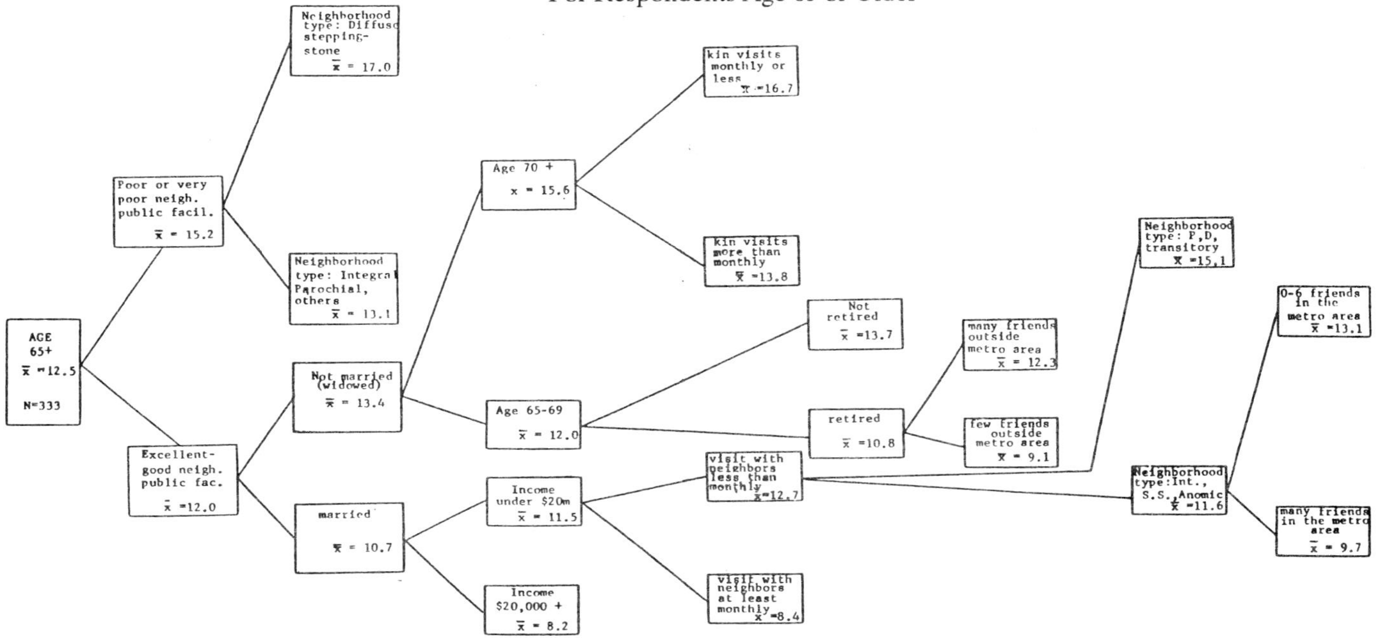

AGE 65+ x̄ =12.5 N=333

Poor or very poor neigh. public facil. x̄ =15.2

Excellent-good neigh. public fac. x̄ =12.0

Neighborhood type: Diffuse stepping-stone x̄ = 17.0

Neighborhood type: Integral Parochial, others x̄ = 13.1

Not married (widowed) x̄ = 13.4

married x̄ = 10.7

Age 70 + x̄ = 15.6

Age 65-69 x̄ = 12.0

Income under $20m x̄ = 11.5

Income $20,000 + x̄ = 8.2

kin visits monthly or less x̄ =16.7

kin visits more than monthly x̄ = 13.8

Not retired x̄ =13.7

retired x̄ =10.8

visit with neighbors monthly x̄ =12.7

visit with neighbors at least monthly x̄ =8.4

many friends outside metro area x̄ = 12.3

few friends outside metro area x̄ = 9.1

Neighborhood type: P,D, transitory x̄ =15.1

Neighborhood type:Int., S.S. x̄ =11.6

0-6 friends in the metro area x̄ =13.1

many friends in the metro area x̄ = 9.7

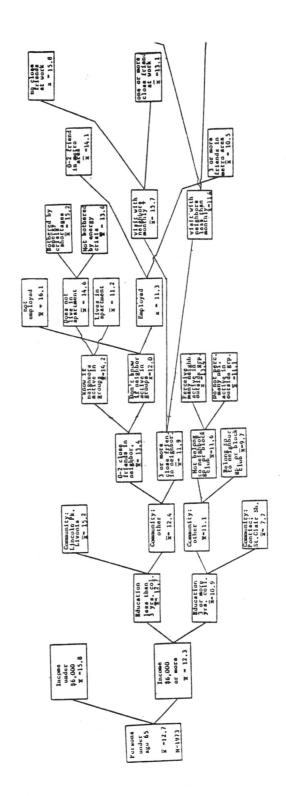

238

CHART XII-2

Automatic Interaction Detection (A.I.D.) Analysis

For Respondents Who Are Under Age 65

TABLE XII-1

Beta Weight Values from the A.I.D. Multivariate Analysis of the RISK score: Neighborhood Variables for Seniors Compared to Non-seniors

	Age 65 or older	Under age 65
Number of voluntary organizations where neighbors are seen	11.3	1.8
Six-fold neighborhood typology	9.6	4.3
Frequency of visiting with neighbors	7.9	5.7
Like the neighborhood	7.1	6.3
Quality of public facilities	4.3	3.4
Number of friends in the neighborhood	3.9	5.3
Perception of neighbors belonging to outside groups	3.9	3.0
Perception that neighbors have things in common	2.0	6.1
Perceived size of neighborhood	1.9	2.7
Belong to block club or neighborhood association	1.1	2.6
Perception that neighbors visit each other	1.0	2.0

ENDNOTES

CHAPTER I

1.   Traditional approaches to social support have developed from social behavior studies of animals and humans. There has been a continuing trend to view social support in terms of some combination of interpersonal ties and helping behaviors that allow individuals to cope with problems and to maintain a state of functional homeostasis. More recently, with a growing emphasis regarding the influence of social stress on health and well-being, some investigators have broadened their scope of study to include the role social support plays in mitigating the effects of stress (cf. Cassel, 1974; Cobb, 1976; Kaplan, Casel, and Gore, 1977).

This new direction, however, has not been systematically developed as pointed out in a recent report to the President's Commission of Mental Health:

> Unfortunately, [social support] studies contain certain conceptual and methodological weaknesses that limit their usefulness with regard to a precise explanation of support systems in disease etiology. Principle among these weaknesses has been a failure of most researchers to relate one set of psychosocial factors (e.g., support systems) to others that have also been shown to influence health, such as stress (1978:180).

Gore (1978) investigated the efforts of social support on health as a result of unemployment. The study involved a two-year longitudinal study of the physical and mental health consequence of involuntary job loss. Social support was operationally defined as 1) the perception of support from spouse, friends, and relatives; 2) frequency of contact with these informal social network participants; and 3) individuals "perceived opportunity for social activities which provide expressive feelings of well-being and a milieu for discussing problems (Gore, 1978:160). Her findings indicate that "levels of social support seem to modify the severity of psychological and health-related responses to unemployment" (1978:163). These levels of social support are identified as "tangible" and "psychological" dimensions of social support which can be interpreted as providing some degree of helping behaviors as well as social-emotional or "expressive" support. She concludes that, consistent with previous research findings, "social support increases coping ability, which is the etiological gate to health and well-being" (1978:157).

Numerous studies and research reviews over the past decade have concluded that the strength of social supports provided by the primary groups of most importance to the individual function as protective factors buffering or cushioning the individual from the physiologic or psychologic consequences of exposure to stress situations. Moss (1973) views social support as a "general social therapy" factory which provides relief from information incongruities. The lack of social support not only enhances one's susceptability to illness, but also directly affects one's feelings of belongingness and well-being. Moss (1973:237) describes the implications of this lack of social support:

> People who do not receive support or who are unable to establish such relationships because they do not know how to go about establishing or maintaining them may have to resort to instrumental accomplishments of various approved goals of communication networks for their feelings of worth, belonging, and self-esteem.

Cassell (1970:195) notes that individuals deprived of "meaningful human contact or group membership" are higher risks for schizophrenia, accidents, suicide, hypertension, and respiratory diseases. In a latter review of the literature, Cassel (1974) pointed out that many investigations of social support have restricted themselves to relating the absence of social support to some stressful situations or disease.

Cassel suggests that efforts should be directed at improving and strengthening the social supports rather than attempting to prevent the stress situation (1974:479). *We agree with this notion and further submit that exposure to stressful situations may lead to "building" "helping networks" within informal social networks. We suggest that encounters with recent problems of life crises will lead to changes within informal support systems. Such changes may expand and strengthen social support efforts, help to maintain existing social supports, or weaken the support network depending on the nature of support (or lack of support) relationships within the social network.* The dissertation by Forest C. W. Graves Jr. (1979) develops this distracting in an empirical fashion from data in the Detroit Study.

2.   For a discussion on the "pathways" approach see Friedson, 1961; Lefton and Rosengren, 1966; and McKinley, 1973.

3.   The work is best summarized in the following references: Kitwak and Meyer, 1966; 1967; Litwak, 1968; Litwak and Meyer, 1974.

CHAPTER III

4.   The RISK index is detailed further in the appendix (B) dealing with its sub-components and operationalization. For the population sampled below age 65 the mean score is 13.9--that is a significant difference and reflects the lower "stress" that has been found in many studies of the aged versus the non-aged. The RISK index also produces a higher average score for women compared to men. This is consistent with many findings that women score higher on "stress" indices partly as a culturally induced pattern. Because of this potential six bias we have elaborated on the sex-linked

differentials and did not include this variable in the multivariate analysis that is discussed in Chapter XII.

CHAPTER VI

5.   See, for example, Warren, 1969; 1971; 1975; 1976; 1979.

CHAPTER VII

6.   The operationalization of the typology is discussed in the general helping network study. (See Warren, 1981.) Appendix C also contains basic information on the construction of the neighborhood types.

7.   See the final report monograph on the helping-network study, Warren, 1976.

CHAPTER VIII

8.   A major analysis was conducted by David Clifford for his doctoral dissertation. See Clifford, 1976.

CHAPTER XII

9.   The work of Durkheim is of course basic to much of present-day sociological theory about community and social organization. His major work on this topic which focuses on the dichotomy of "mechanical" versus "organic" social cohesion is the *Division of Labor in Society*. See Durkheim (1964).

APPENDIX A

DETAILED ANALYSIS OF THE RECENT CONCERN OF "THINKING HOW IT WOULD BE TO RETIRE"

APPENDIX TABLE A-1

Thought How it Would be to Retire

Thought about retirement within the last month	29.1%
a) Talked to someone	18.9
b) Did not talk	10.2
Thought about retirement longer ago than the last month	26.4%
Have never thought about retirement	42.5%
Not ascertained	1.9%
TOTAL	99.9%
	N = 2453

APPENDIX TABLE A-2

Thinking About Retirement by Respondent Age

	Within the last month	Talked to Someone about it	Did not talk to anyone	
Under Age 30	21.8%	11.2%	10.6%	N-454
Age 30 - 39	25.6%	14.8%	10.8%	N-520
Age 40 - 49	39.0%	25.5%	13.5%	N-526
Age 50 - 59	46.0%	33.6%	12.4%	N-452
Age 60 - 64	33.3%	24.7%	8.7%	N-156
Age 65 - 69	8.1%	3.7%	4.4%	N-141
Age 70 or Older	2.6%	2.6%	0.0%	N-190
TOTAL	29.1%	18.9%	10.2%	N-2439

APPENDIX TABLE A-3

Thinking about How it Would be to Retire

	Had concern in 1974, within the last month, and talked to someone about it	Had concern in 1974, within the last month, and did not talk to anyone about it
Had concern in 1975 within the last month	59.7%	48.4%
Had concern in period since 1974 interview	17.4%	20.0%
Did not have concern in 1975	22.8%	31.6%
Total	99.9%	100.0%
	N = 322	N = 155

APPENDIX TABLE A-4

Helping Networks and the Issue of Retirement

	Number of different kinds of helpers	Number of different kinds of helping behaviors
None	35.1	35.1
One	33.6	20.3
Two	11.7	16.4
Three	8.4	8.8
Four	4.5	5.9
Five	3.2	2.7
Six or more	2.5	9.5
Not ascertained	1.0	1.4
TOTAL	100.0%	100.1%

N = 715

Mean number of helpers	1.31	Mean number of helping behaviors per helper	1.95

APPENDIX TABLE A-5

Kind of Helpers Used in Dealing with the
Recent Concern of Thinking How it Would be to Retire

	Percent of those experiencing problem in last month
Spouse	79%
Friend	35%
Co-worker	32%
Relative	29%
Neighbor	18%
Formal helpers	8%
doctor	5%
teacher	2%
clergy	1%
counselor [*]	1%

N = 457

[*] Counselor includes social worker, psychologist, and psychiatrist.

APPENDIX TABLE A-6

Helpers Used by Persons who Will Retire in 1975 verus Other Respondents in Regard to the Recent Concern of Thinking About How it Would be to Retire (1974 Baseline Survey)

	Will retire in 1975	Other non-retired respondents	
	Percent using each helper		Percent difference
	A	B	(A - B)
Spouse	72%	79% +	− 9%
Friend	50% +	34% −	+ 47%
Co-worker	53% +	23% −	+ 130%
Relative	47% +	28% −	+ 68%
Neighbor	35% +	17% −	+ 106%
Formal helpers	17% +	8% −	+ 113%
	(N = 40)	(N = 2103)	
Use no helpers	5%	36%	
Percent having this concern	48%	33%	

APPENDIX B
OPERATIONALIZATION OF RISK MEASURE

APPENDIX B
OPERATIONALIZATION OF RISK MEASURE

To address the question of consequences of helping on the well-being of the person seeking help, a set of three subscales and a summary scale were devised based upon a simple additive score for a series of interview items contained in both the 1974 and 1975 schedules. These items were grouped into the following categories to form indices: "Depressed Mental Outlook (DMO); Psychosomatic Complaint; Perceived ILL Health." Finally, the scores for the individual on each of these three scales were added together and utilized as a comprehensive index of "risk to well-being". (RISK)

Items for the DMO index are as follows:

"Felt so 'blue' or 'low' it ruined your whole day.

Felt it's no use trying to do things because so many things go wrong.

Have there ever been times when you couldn't take care of things because you just couldn't get going?"

The first two items are contained in part of the list of nine "recent concerns" while the third item is contained in a list of symptoms elsewhere in the interview. Depending on the frequency of reported occurrence of these feelings, a scale was constructed by adding the values of each item to form a score ranging from 0 to 22. For the total population interviewed in 1974, the mean score for DMO is 5.882 with a standard deviation of 5.381.

A second scale focuses on psychosomatic complaint. The items used to construct this score are as follows:

"People often have tension headaches or similar complaints.

Have you ever felt tension in this way?

Do you ever have any trouble getting to sleep or staying asleep?

Have you ever been bothered by nervousness, feeling fidgity, and tense?

Have you ever had spells or dizziness?"

These items--derived and modified--have been utilized in a number of studies including the Gurin-Veroff study of 1960, "How Americans View

Their Mental Health." Using the reported frequency of these symptoms, a score ranging from 0 to 20 was constructed. The mean score for the sample is 5.073 with a standard deviation of 4.496.

The third index constructed as a dependent variable measure of helping is "perceived ill health." It consists simply of two items linked in an additive fashion. These are the following:

a) "Now we have a few questions about your overall health. How was your health been over the last year or so? Would you say you've been in *poor health, fair health, good health, or excellent health*?

b) Has any ill health affected the amount of work you do?"

Scoring of the values for these items provides a score range from 0 to 20 with a sample mean occurrence of 4.609 and a standard deviation of 4.821.

An additional overall measure of the "well-being" of the individual is derived by adding the scores of each of the three indices to form an index of "risk to well being" which we shall refer to subsequently in the analysis as simply "RISK." The score could range form 0 to 62. On this measure, the sample population has a mean score of 15.587 and a standard deviation of 10.335 (N = 2429).

No specific design provision was made for the validation of the subscales or the overall RISK scale. However, in the second wave of data collection in 1975, two items were added to the interview which were aimed at providing a direct, behavioral report which would be a measure of "stress" or well-being. These questions were as follows:

"In the last several weeks have you made any extra doctor's or dentist's appointments to take car of a health problem you've put off checking into until now?

In the last several weeks have you gotten any extra medicines at the pharmacy or drug store to help you relax?"

For the first of these items, 13.3% of the sample responded in the affirmative, while 9.4% so indicated for the second item.

In Table B-1, the gamma values for the two items on extra medical appointments and medicines to relax are shown for the relation of each item to the four dependent variables of mental and physical well-being. In all instances modest to strong values obtain. In particular, the relation to the "medicine to relax" item are high for all four measures--with the +.56 value for RISK twice that for the item on extra medical appointments--+.28.

APPENDIX TABLE B-1

RELATIONSHIP BETWEEN WELL-BEING MEASURES AND MAKING EXTRA MEDICAL APPOINTMENTS AND TAKING MEDICATION TO RELAX

	"In the last several weeks have you made any extra doctor's or dentist's appointments to take care of a health problem you've put off checking into until now?"	"In the last several weeks have you gotten any extra medicines at the pharmacy or drug store to help you relax?"
Depressed mental outlook	+.23[*]	+.47
Psychosomatic complaint	+.30	+.51
Perceived ill health	+.25	+.51
Risk to well-being	+.28	+.56
	N = 1626	

*Gamma values

APPENDIX C
OPERATIONALIZATION OF THE NEIGHBORHOOD TYPE

APPENDIX C
OPERATIONALIZATION OF THE
NEIGHBORHOOD TYPE

A total of 59 elementary school districts are included in the "neighborhood sample." These units were included partly as a result of previous research on the same locales and partly to provide a comparison of suburban and central city neighborhoods. In drawing the sample of school districts--both in the earlier study and those added from the eight non-Detroit communities--no measurement of the social organization of the neighborhood was utilized.

The basic dimensions of the neighborhood of the typology are three attributes that were operationalized in the present investigation and then dichotomized to provide the classificatory schema. The variables composing this schema include: 1) level of reference group commitment to the neighborhood, 2) amount of informal and formal social interaction, and 3) the associational or other ties to the larger community.

Reference Group of the Neighborhood

The survey instrument contains several questions which ask about how the individual feels about their neighborhood. This includes commitment to stay versus plans to move, how much they feel they have in common with their neighbors, and the negative and positive qualities of the neighborhood. It is possible to consider each of these subdimensions:

  All of these ....
  Some other idea (what?)..............................
  Don/t know...

Where the individual selected an alternative of a "larger area" or "some other idea" they were than asked, "What streets or roads would be the boundaries?" A score range of 0 to 2 was developed. "All of these," and the block or small unit was given a value of "1", "walking distance" or a description of boundaries corresponding to an area only 20% larger than the sample elementary school district received a "2" score. If a larger area was described, a zero score was given as was the case for a "don"t know" response.

The distribution of response on the perceived neighborhood boundary closely approximates findings from the earlier study carried out in 1969.

For the sum of items and the values assigned to particular response categories, the "reference dimension" had a range form 0 to 11.

APPENDIX TABLES

APPENDIX TABLE II-1

**Comparison of Helping-Network Sample Age Distribution
with the 1970 Census Data for the Detroit SMSA**

	Helping Network sample (1974)	U.S. Census for Detroit SMSA (1970)
Age 20 to 29	18.2	23.5
Age 30 to 39	20.8	18.1
Age 40 to 49	21.0	21.3
Age 50 to 59	18.1	17.5
Age 60 to 69	11.8	11.1
Age 60 to 64	6.2	6.2
Age 65 to 69	5.6	4.9
Age 70 or older	10.1	8.5
Percent age 65+	15.7	13.4
TOTAL	100.0%	100.0%

(N=2486)

APPENDIX TABLE II-2

Interviewer Report of Respondent Attitude

"How suspicious did R seem to be about the study before the interview?"

	70 or older	65-69	60-64	under 60
Not at all	69%	70%	72%	83%
Somewhat	26	23	22	15
Very suspicious	6	7	6	3
TOTAL	101%	100%	100%	101%

"Compared to other R's you have interviewed in this study, how well did R understand the questions in the interview?"

	70 or older	65-69	60-64	under 60
Above average for most R's	8%	15%	21%	30%
Average for most R's	66	67	66	62
Below average for most R's	26	18	13	9
TOTAL	100%	100%	100%	101%

APPENDIX TABLE II-3

Race of Respondents in Each Analysis Grouping

	White	Black	Oriental	Total
Retired more than 1 year before interview	74%	26%	0%	100%
Retired within the last year	32%	65%	4%	101%
To retire within 1 year after interview	88%	13%	0%	101%
Other persons interviewed	80%	20%	1%	101%

APPENDIX TABLE II-4

Sex of Respondent for the Four Groups

	Male	Female	Total
Retired before 1974	56%	44%	100%
Retired in 1974	50	50	100%
Retired in 1975	43	57	100%
Other respondents	45	55	100%

APPENDIX TABLE II-5

Number of Persons Employed in the Respondents' Household

	Retired more than 1 year before interview	Retired within the last year	To retire within 1 year after interview	Other persons inter-viewed
None	90%	85%	3%	13%
One	9	13	63	61
Two or more	1	2	35	26
TOTAL	100%	100%	101%	100%

APPENDIX TABLE II-6

Economic Constraints due to the Recession

	Retired more than 1 year before interview	Retired within the last year	To retire within 1 year after interview	Other persons inter-viewed
Cutting back on buying	41%	50%+	43%	46%
Using up savings	44%	63%+	45%	54%+
Can't save as much as usual	63%	75%+	70%+	63%
Cut back on vacations and travel	43%	50%+	38%−	47%
Done more household work and laundry yourself rather than pay	23%	19%	30%+	23%
Done your own painting and house repairs	20%	13%	35%+	30%+
Gone out less to shows and restaurants	34%−	63%+	50%	48%
Cut back on money spent for clothing	42%	63%+	40%	51%
Tried to economize more than usual on food bills	54%−	75%+	63%	73%+

APPENDIX TABLE II-7

Length of Time Living in the Same City

	Retired more than 1 year before interview	Retired within the last year	To retire within 1 year after interview	Other persons inter-viewed
2 years or less	9%	6%	3%	22%
3 to 5 years	9	19	3	23
5+ to 10 years	13	19	15	17
10+ to 19 years	20	22	35	23
20 years or more	48	35	45	15
TOTAL	99%	101%	101%	100%

APPENDIX TABLE II-8

Report of Plans to Move from Residence

	Retired more than 1 year before interview	Retired within the last year	To retire within 1 year after interview	Other persons inter-viewed
Plan to move within one year	4%	2%	8%	13%
Plan to move within five years or longer	4	10	23	20
No plans to move	92	88	69	68
TOTAL	100%	100%	100%	101%

APPENDIX TABLE III-1

Perceived Spheres of Problems for Respondents
"What do you think are some of the most serious problems facing people in this community?"

	No problems	Crime	Work	Family	Economic
Retired more than 1 year before interview	22%	29%	7%	0%	43%
Retired within the last year	17%	41%+	7%	0%	35%
To retire within 1 year after interview	8%	40%+	10%	3%	40%
Other persons interviewed	17%	24%	6%	1%	52%

APPENDIX TABLE III-2

Total Number of Life Crises Events
1974 Pattern

	None	One	Two or more	Total
Retired more than 1 year before interview	48%	37%	15%	100%
Retired within the last year	0%*	58%	43%	101%
To retire within 1 year after interview	33%	45%	23%	101%
Other persons interviewed	34%	33%	33%	100%

*Since retirement in the last year is one of the life crises this group could not have a zero category. By 1975, this same group had 31 percent with zero life crises, 25 percent with one, and 44 percent with two or more.

APPENDIX TABLE IV-1

Use of Hospitals and Clinics in Relation to Having
a Friend working in that Setting

	Retired more than 1 year before interview	Retired within the last year	To retire within 1 year after interview	Other persons inter-viewed
Use a clinic or hospital in the last year or so for "the kinds of problems we having been talking about"	26%	23%	35%+	30%
Have a friend who works in a clinic or hospital	10%	12%	25%	18%
Difference	16%+	11%	10%	12%
Ratio	2.6:1	1.9:1	1.4:1	1.7:1

APPENDIX TABLE IV-2

Use of Formal Helpers in Dealing with Life Crises
(1975 Follow-up)

	Retired more than 1 year before interview	Retired within the last year	To retire within 1 year after interview	Other persons inter- viewed
Doctor	57%	45%	38%	50%
Clergy	11%	45%	18%	15%
Police	5%	18%	3%	9%
Teacher	1%	0%	5%	6%
Counselor*	0%	0%	5%	5%
TOTAL	74%	108%	69%	85%

*Counselor includes social worker, psychiatrist, and psychologist.

APPENDIX TABLE IV-3

Perceived Helpfulness of Different Helpers
for Personal Problems
(1975 Follow-up Interview)

	Retired more than 1 year before interview	Retired within the last year	To retire within 1 year after interview	Other persons inter-viewed
	Percent "very helpful"[*]			
Spouse	81%+	75%	74%	71%
Relative	45%	39%	42%	33%
Friend	22%	43%+	28%	25%
Co-worker	26%+	0%−	23%	16%
Neighbor	21%	25%	16%−	13%
Doctor	45%	60%+	61%+	39%
Clergy	43%	44%	52%+	35%
Police	28%	0%−	38%	27%
Psychologist +	0%	0%	0%	36%
Teacher +	16%	0%	31%+	32%
Social worker +	0%	0%	0%	25%

[*]The specific questioned asked was: "From your own experience, how helpful are the following kinds of people when there is something on your mind that you need to talk over-- something personal that you are concerned about?"

APPENDIX TABLE V-1

What is Most Helpful When Person Goes for Help?
(1975)

	Retired more than 1 year before interview	Retired within the last year	To retire within 1 year after interview	Other persons interviewed
Someone who listens, a shoulder to cry on	25%−	39%	55%+	47%
Someone who discusses the problem, asks questions, argues with me, helps me think it through, takes action	16	15	10	15
Some who is sympathetic, calming, non-judgmental, discrete, patient	13	0	18	12
Someone who is experienced, tells me what they did under similar circumstances	2	8	0	2
Someone who gives advice--tells me what to do, takes action, tells me who else to talk to	19	15	8−	18
Someone who does something else	2	0	0	1
Nothing--I don't go to anyone with my problems	24	23	8−	6−
TOTAL	101%	100%	99%	101%

APPENDIX TABLE VI-1

"In general, how do you feel about this neighborhood?"

	Retired more than 1 year before interview	Retired within the last year	To retire within 1 year after interview	Other persons inter-viewed
A good place to live	65%	37%−	60%	62%
A fairly good place to live	29	54	35	32
A poor place to live	6	6	5	4
A very poor place to live	1	4	0	1
TOTAL	101%	101%	100%	99%

APPENDIX TABLE VI-2

"How would you describe the general quality of public facilities and services in the immediate vincinity of the respondents' home?"

	Retired more than 1 year before interview	Retired within the last year	To retire within 1 year after interview	Other persons inter-viewed
Excellent[*]	32%	24% −	26% −	37%
Good	53	57	59	50
Fair	12	19	15	12
Poor	3	0	0	2
TOTAL	100%	100%	100%	101%

[*]The specific details for each category are:

EXCELLENT--STREET LIGHTS, UTILITIES, STREETS SIGNS ARE NEW OR IN PERFECAT CONDITION AND LACK OF RUBBISH IN ALLEYS AND STREET IS OUTSTANDING. STREETS AND ROADS ARE IN EXCELLENT CONDITION.

GOOD--PUBLIC SERVICES APPEAR TO BE MAINTAINED, STREETS AND ROADS ARE IN GOOD CONDITION. THERE IS LITTLE DAMAGE TO STREET LIGHTS, GARBAGE IS NOT SCATTERED AROUND, ALTHOUGH SOME EQUIPMENT MAY NEED REPLACEMENT.

FAIR--SOME STREET LIGHTS ARE INADEQUATE, STREET SIGNS ARE IN POOR CONDITION, THERE IS SOME LITTER IN THE ALLEYS OR STREETS. STREETS AND ROADS NEED REPAIR.

POOR--BROKEN AND DEFECTIVE PUBLIC EQUIPMENT IS QUITE EVIDENT AND TYPICAL OF THE AREA, LITTER IS SCATTERED IN THE STREET AND THE OVERALL APPEARANCE OF THE STREET IS UNCLEAN.

APPENDIX TABLE VI-3

Comparison of Respondent Dwelling Unit to Others
on the Block: Age, Interior and Exterior Upkeep

(Interviewers' Evaluation)

	Age (25 years or more)	Interior (very well)	Exterior (very well)	Total Discrepancy
		Percent Difference[*]		
Retired more than 1 year before interview	−5%	+19%	+14%	38%
Retired within the last year	−4%	+11%	+21%	36%
To retire within 1 year after interview	−3%	+9%	+12%	24%
Other persons interviewed	−1%	+10%	+6%	17%

[*]Based on comparing respondent to block. A negative figure means that respondent percentage was greater than "other houses" on the block. Positive figure indicates that respondent percentage was smaller than that for "other houses on the block."

APPENDIX TABLE VI-4

Percent of Time Neighbors are Seen in
Organizations Respondent Belongs

	Retired more than 1 year before interview	Retired within the last year	To retire within 1 year after interview	Other persons inter-viewed
Church or synagogue	41%	55%	62%+	41%
Church-connected groups	17%	15%	28%+	16%
Labor unions	7%	4%	13%	10%
Fraternal lodges or veterans' groups	5%	2%	13%+	7%
Civic groups	2%	0%	8%+	6%+
Professional groups	1%	2%	5%	3%
Youth-oriented groups (scouts, little league)	1%	2%	8%+	12%+
Community centers	4%	2%	3%	5%
Neighborhood improvement associations, block clubs or homeowners groups	14%	19%	13%	14%
Social or cards playing groups or country clubs	7%	4%	8%	10%
Sports teams	2%	0%	10%+	11%+
Nationality or ethnic groups	1%	0%	3%	2%
Political clubs or organizations	1%	0%	3%	3%
Social action groups	1%	0%	8%+	2%
Charity or welfare organizations	2%	0%	13%+	4%

APPENDIX TABLE VI-5

Balance of Neighbor to Non-neighbor Contacts
in Organizations

	Retired more than 1 year before interview	Retired within the last year	To retire within 1 year after interview	Other persons inter-viewed
Church or synagogue	+	+	+ +	+
Church–connected groups	+	+	+	+
Labor unions	–	–	–	–
Fraternal lodges or veterans' groups	–	–	–	–
Civic groups	–	–	+	+
Professional groups	–	–	–	–
Youth–oriented groups (scouts, little league)	+ +	+ +	+	+ +
Community centers	–	+	–	+ +
Neighborhood improvement associations, block clubs or homeowners group	+ +	+ +	+ +	+ +
Social or cards playing groups or country clubs	–	+	+	+
Sports teams	+	–	+	+
Nationality or ethnic groups	–	–	–	–
Political clubs or organizations	–	–	+ +	+ +
Social action groups	–	–	+ +	–
Charity or welfare organizations	–	–	+ +	+

Key:
+ + = 75% or more neighbor contact
+ = 50% to 74% neighbor contact
– = less than 50% neighbor contact

APPENDIX TABLE VII-1

**Neighborhood Type in Relation to Kinds of
Helping Behaviors used by Persons
65 Years of Age or Older**

	Listening	Asking questions	Showing a new way	Referring	Taking action
Integral	68%	44%	7%	20%	25%
Parochial	66%	57%	14%	14%	14%
Diffuse	67%	40%	33%	33%	25%
Stepping stone	94%	47%	30%	36%	36%
Transitory	82%	47%	18%	18%	18%
Anomic	92%	46%	37%	8%	11%

APPENDIX TABLE VII-2

Neighborhood Type in Relation to Individual and Collective Mutual Aid in the Neighborhood as Perceived by Persons Age 65 or Older

	People keep an eye on each others' houses when you go away	People will help with personal problems and car	There is someone to rely on for home repairs
Integral	91%	67%	17%
Parochial	85%	59%	29%+
Diffuse	90%	83%+	30%+
Stepping stone	88%	71%	9%−
Transitory	88%	38%−	16%
Anomic	90%	63%	15%

APPENDIX TABLE VIII-2

Type of Helping Behavior in Relation to High versus Medium and Low Helping Strength Cities for Persons Age 65 or Older

Percent with one or more concerns

	Strong	Medium-Weak
Just listens	73%	76%
Asks questions	36%	29%
Shows a new way to look at the problem	36%+	24%+
Refers	27%+	12%−
Takes action	27%	18%
	(N=11)	(N=17)

APPENDIX TABLE X-1

**The Differential Use of Spouse, Kin, Friends
and Neighbors for Selected Recent Concerns:
Retired and Non-Retired Persons**

	All retired persons	Non−retired persons
Crime in the local neighborhood	33% − 54%*	30% − 62%
	21	32
Thinking about moving because of crime	33% − 88%	32% − 73%
	55	41
Feel like "it's no use trying to do things"	55% − 45%	65% − 18%
	10	47
Feel so "low" it ruined your whole day	23% − 63%	59% − 15%
	40	44

*highest and lowest percent of help from one of the four kinds of informal helpers.

APPENDIX TABLE X-2

Change in the Kind of Help Provided by Particular Helpers for Recent Concerns: Four Analysis of Retirement Groups

	Retired more than 1 year before interview	Retired within the last year	To retire within 1 year after interview	Other persons inter- viewed
Just listens				
spouse	−	+	+	−
relative	−	+		
friend				
neighbor			+	
Asks questions				
spouse		−		
relative		−	+	
friend		−		
neighbor		−	+	+
Shows a new way				
spouse				
relative				+
friend		+		
neighbor				
Referral				
spouse		+	−	
relative	+	+	−	−
friend				+
neighbor	+	+	−	−
Takes action				
spouse				+
relative	+	−	+	−
friend				
neighbor		−		
Total differences	5	12	8	8 = 33
Non-neighbor	4	9	6	6 = 25

APPENDIX TABLE X-3

Change in the Kind of Help Provided by Particular Helpers for Life Crises: Four Analyses of Retirement Groups

	Retired more than 1 year before interview	Retired within the last year	To retire within 1 year after interview	Other persons interviewed
Listens				
relative*		−		
friend				
neighbor				
Asks questions				
relative				
friend		+		
neighbor	−			+
Shows a new way				
relative		+		
friend				
neighbor		−		
Refers				
relative		+	−	−
friend		+		
neighbor		+		
Takes action				
relative				
friend				+
neighbor				
Total differences	1	7	1	3 = 12

*Includes spouse.

APPENDIX TABLE X-4

**Variability between Helpers in the Type of Help
Provided in Relation to the Four Retirement Groups**

	Retired more than 1 year before interview	Retired within the last year	To retire within 1 year after interview	Other persons inter-viewed
		Recent Concerns		
Listens-range[*]	27	8	23	6
Asks questions	2	31	22	3
Shows a new way	7	49	6	11
Refers	24	19	15	14
Takes action-range	11	0	8	13
Total	71	107	74	47
		Life Crises		
Listens-range	4	15	5	2
Asks questions	26	21	8	1
Shows a new way	5	33	8	8
Refers-range	20	28	16	7
Takes action-range	15	0	6	8
Total	70	97	43	26

APPENDIX TABLE X-5

Matching of Who Helps and How
They Help for Life Crises

− Relative-friend:	lowest matching for those retired more than 1 year and those about to retire; highest matching of type of help for those not approaching retirement
− Relative-neighbor:	little change by retirement status in matching of who helps: highest matching of type of help for those not approaching retirement
+ + Neighbor-friend:	steady increase in matching with highest for those retired for 1 year or more; lowest matching of type of help for those newly retired; highest for persons not approaching retirement
− Range-relative, friend, neighbor:	no significant variations in who helps; those newly retired have lowest matching of type of help; those not approaching retirement have highest matching

APPENDIX TABLE XI-1

Zero Order Correlations among Different Kinds of Helpers
Used in Coping with Recent Concerns: Persons
65 or older versus those 65 or less

Upper right triangle: Aged 65 or older — Lower left triangle: Under age 65

	Spouse	Relative	Friend	Neighbor	Co-worker	clergy	Police	Doctor	Counselor	Teacher
Spouse		+.99*	+.01	+.01	+.01	.00	+.01	+.01	.00	.00
Relative	+.79*		+.03	+.02	.00	+.03	.00	.00	-.01	-.01
Friend	+.12	+.13		+.56*	+.25*	+.37*	+.11	+.44*	+.02	+.09
Neighbor	+.09	+.10	+.45*		+.08	+.26*	+.24*	+.45*	+.13	-.02
Co-worker	+.09	+.07	+.44*	+.30*		+.18*	+.23*	-.02	+.47*	+.31*
clergy	+.03	+.06	+.21*	+.26*	+.16*		+.15	+.24*	+.09	+.21*
police	+.05	+.04	+.19*	+.27*	+.16*	+.21*		-.03	-.02	-.01
Doctor	+.06	+.07	+.30*	+.25*	+.13	+.27*	+.05		-.01	-.01
Counselor	+.04	+.03	+.17*	+.18*	+.16*	+.31*	+.12	+.21*		+.50*
Teacher	+.04	+.04	+.21*	+.22*	+.22*	+.32*	+.21*	+.12	+.16*	

Number of significant coefficients: 65 or older = 15/45 = 33%

under 65 = 25/45 = 56%

APPENDIX TABLE XI-2

Types of Organizations Respondent Belongs To

	Retired more than 1 year before interview	Retired within the last year	To retire within 1 year after interview	Other persons inter-viewed
Church or synagogue	75%	77%	83%	69%
Church-connected groups	30%	23%	48%	27%
Labor unions	33%	21%	43%	40%
Fraternal lodges or veterans' groups	20%	15%	30%	19%
Civic groups	5%	6%	13%	10%
Professional groups	7%	6%	18%	16%
Youth-oriented groups (scouts, little league)	1%	2%	13%	16%
Community centers	9%	4%	8%	6%
Neighborhood improvement associations, block clubs or homeowners ggroups	16%	23%+	13%	16%
Social or card playing groups or country clubs	17%	8%	13%	19%
Sport teams	4%	2%	18%	22%
Nationality or ethnic groups	4%	2%	8%	5%
Political clubs or organizations	4%	0%	3%	4%
Social action groups	4%	4%	10%	5%
Charity or welfare organizations	5%	4%	15%	8%

APPENDIX TABLE XI-3

Being an Officer and Knowing Leaders
of an Organization

	Retired more than 1 year before interview	Retired within the last year	To retire within 1 year after interview	Other persons inter- viewed
		Percent "Yes"		
Do you now hold an official position of leadership or serve as an officer for any...groups?	15%	16%	21%	21%
Do you happen to know anyone in this neighborhood who is an officer or very active in an organization or club?	20%	27%	28%	33%
TOTAL	35%	43%	49%	54%

APPENDIX TABLE XI-4

Sources of Information for "Dealing with the Kinds of Problems we have Talked About"

	Retired more than 1 year before interview	Retired within the last year	To retire within 1 year after interview	Other persons inter-viewed
	Percent "very helpful"			
TV commentators	65%+	65%+	56%	59%
TV specials	68%	76%+	44%−	71%
Radio	60%	77%+	56%	49%−
Newspapers	78%	83%+	67%−	76%
Magazines	50%	72%+	44%−	63%+
Opinion polls	41%	65%+	22%−	40%
Someone in your union	23%	31%+	13%−	22%
Someone in an organization	29%−	73%+	43%	35%
Relatives	62%	78%+	67%	60%
Friends not living in the neighborhood	47%−	78%+	33%−	57%
Friends living in the neighborhood	45%	78%+	22%−	49%
Friends at work	15%−	25%	63%+	40%

APPENDIX TABLE XI–5

**Reported Voting in the Presidential Election
in Relation to Perceived Size of Neighborhood
For Persons Age 65 or Older**

	Voted in 1972
People right next door or across the street	82%
People on my block	81%
People within walking distance	93%+
A larger unit	85%

APPENDIX TABLE XII-1

**Beta Weight Values from the A.I.D. Multivariate
Analysis of the RISK Score: Seniors
Compared to Non-seniors**

	Age 65 or older	Under age 65
<u>Demographics</u>		
Martial status	7.1	5.2
Income	7.0	6.1
Employment	6.6	0.8
Age	5.4	4.7
Education	3.1	5.1
Race	2.9	6.4
TOTAL	32.1	28.3
<u>Non−neighborhood</u> <u>Social Ties:</u>		
Number of groups belong to	10.3	3.2
See kin	8.3	2.3
Number of friends beyond metro area	6.2	4.1
Number of friends in metro area	5.9	4.4
Number of relatives	4.9	5.3
See friends	2.4	1.2
Number of co− worker friends	2.3	7.5
TOTAL	40.3	28.0

APPENDIX TABLE XII-2

Beta Weight Values from the A.I.D. Multivariate Analysis of the RISK score: Neighborhood Variables for Seniors Compared to Non-seniors

	Age 65 or older	Under age 65
Number of voluntary organizations where neighbors are seen	11.3	1.8
Six-fold neighborhood typology	9.6	4.3
Frequency of visiting with neighbors	7.9	5.7
Like the neighborhood	7.1	6.3
Quality of public facilities	4.3	3.4
Number of friends in the neighborhood	3.9	5.3
Perception of neighbors belonging to outside groups	3.9	3.0
Perception that neighbors have things in common	2.0	6.1
Perceived size of neighborhood	1.9	2.7
Belong to block club or neighborhood association	1.1	2.6
Perception that neighbors visit each other	1.0	2.0
TOTAL	54.0	43.2

REFERENCES AND BIBLIOGRAPHY

Abrahams, Ruby, B. "Mutual Helping Styles of Caregiving in a Mutual Aid Program--The Widowed Service Line", In Kaplan and Killian (1976): 245-259.

Adams, Bert. *Kinship in an Urban Setting*. Chicago: Markham Publishing Company, 1968.

Angell, Robert. "The Moral Integration of American Cities." *American Journal of Sociology* 57, July 1951, pp. 1-140.

Applier, D., K. Lynch, and J. R. Meyer. *The View from the Road*. Massachusetts: MIT Press, 1964.

Arno, M., and D. Schwartz. *Community Mental Health: Reflections and Explorations*. Flushing, New York: Spectrum Publication, 1974.

Arrow, Kenneth J. *The Limits of Organization*. New York: W. W. Norton, 1974.

Austin, David M. "Influence of Community Setting On Neighborhood Action." In John B. Turner (ed.), *Neighborhood Organization for Community Action*. National Association of Social Work, 1968, pp. 76-105.

Bales, Freed and Talcott Parsons. *Interaction Process Analysis*. New York: The Free Press, 1955.

Berger, Peter L., and Ricard J. Neuhaus. *To Empower People: The Role of Mediating Structures in Public Policy*. Washington, D.C.: American Enterprise Institute, 1977.

Black, K. Dean, and Vern L. Bengtson. "Implications of Telecommunications Technology for Old People." In Marvin Sussman and E. Shanas (eds.), *Family Bureaucracy and the Elderly*. Durham, North Carolina: Duke University Press, 1977, pp. 162-196.

Blau, Peter M., and W. Richard Scott. *Formal Organizations: A Comparative Approach*. San Francisco: Chandler Publishing Company, 1962.

Blaut, J. M., and D. Stea. "Place Learning" *Place Perception Research Reports*. No. 4. Massachusetts: Clark University, 1969.

Blum, Alan. "Social Structure, Social Class and Participation in Primary Relationships." In Arthur Shostak and William Gomberg (eds.), *Blue Collar World*. Englewood Cliffs, New Jersey: Prentice Hall, 1964, pp. 145-207.

Bott, Elizabeth. *Family and Social Network: Roles, Norms and External Relationships in Ordinary Urban Families.* London: Tavistock Publications, 1957.

Brieger, Robert L. "Career Attributes and Network Structure: A Blockmodel Study of Biomedical Research Specialty." *American Sociological Review*, 41, February 1976, pp. 117-135.

Briggs, R. "Urban Cognative Distance." Unpublished Doctoral Dissertation, Ohio State University, 1971.

Broskowski, Anthony, and Frank Baker. "Professional, Organizational, and Social Barriers to Primary Prevention." *American Journal of Orthopsychiatry* 44, October 1974, pp. 707-719.

Brown, Bertram S. "Obstacles to Treatment for Blue Collar Workers." *New Dimensions in Mental Health.* Report from the Director, National Institute of Mental Health, Public Health Service, June 1976.

Bryan, James, and Mary Test,. "Models and Helping: Naturalistic Studies in Aiding Behavior." *Journal of Personality and Special Psychology* 6, August 1967, pp. 400-407.

Cantor, Marjorie H., and Mary J. Mayer. "Factors in Differential Utilization of Services by Urban Elderly." *Journal of Gerontological Social Work*, Volume I (1), Fall 1978, pp. 47-61.

Cantor, Marjorie H. "Neighbors and Friends: An Overlooked Resource in the Informal Support System." Paper Presented at a Symposium on Natural Support Systems for the Elderly at the 30th Annual Meeting of the Gerontological Society, San Francisco, California, November 20, 1977.

Caplan, Gerald. "Support Systems." Keynote Address to Conference of Psychiatry, Rutgers Medical School and New Jersey Mental Health Association on June 8, 1972 at Newark, New Jersey.

_____. "Support Stystems." In *Support System and Community Mental Health*, pp. 1-40. Edited by Gerald Caplan. New York: Behavioral Publications, 1974.

Cassel, J. C. "Psychosocial Processes and 'stress': Theoretical Formulation." *International Journal of Health Services* 4 (3) (1974) 471-482.

Clark, Terry. "Community or Communities." In *Community Structure and Decision Making: Comparative Analysis*, pp. 83-90. Edited by Terry Clark. San Francisco, California: Chandler Publishing Company, 1968.

Clifford, David L. *A Comparative Study of Helping Patterns in Eight Urban Communities*. University of Michigan Doctoral Dissertation, 1976.

Collins, A. H. "Natural Delivery Systems: Accessible Sources of Power for Mental Health." *American Journal of Orthopsychiatry*, (43) (1973): 46-52.

Collins, Alice H., and Diane I. Pancoast. *Natural Helping Networks: A Strategy for Prevention*. New York: National Association of Social Workers, Washington, D. C., 1976.

Cooley, Charles Horton, Robert C. Angell and L. J. Carr. *Introductory Sociology*. New York: Schribners, 1933.

_____. *Social Organization*. New York: Scribners, 1966.

Craik, K. H. "Environment Psychology." In Craik, K. H., *et al.*, (eds.), *New Directions in Psychology*. New York: Holt Publishers, 1970.

Craven, Paul and Barry Wellman. "Informal Interpersonal Relations and Social Networks." *Sociological Inquiry*, 43, Nos. 3 and 4 (1973): 57-88.

Croog, Sydney, Alberta Lipson, and Soll Levine. "Help Patterns in Severe Illness: Non-Family Resources, and Institutions." *Journal of Marriage and the Family* 34, February 1973, pp. 32-41.

Crump, Barry N. "The Portability of Urban Ties." Unpublished paper, Centre for Urban and Community Studies, University of Toronto, 1977.

Cumming, Elaine. *Systems of Social Regulation*. New York: Atherton Press, 1968.

Davis, James, Joe Spaeth, and Carolyn Huson. "A Technique for Analyzing the Effects of Group Composition." *American Sociological Review* 26, April 1961, pp. 215-225.

Davis, Kingsley. *Human Society*. New York: The MacMillan Company, 1948.

Dono, John E., Cecilia M. Falbe, *et al.* "The Structure and Function of Primary Groups in Old Age." Paper Delivered at the Annual Meeting of the American Sociological Association, San Francisco, California, 1978.

Farley, Reynolds. "The Changing Distribution of Negroes within Metropolitan Areas: The Emergence of Black Suburbs." *American Journal of Sociology*, 75, Number 4, Part 1, January, pp. 512-529.

Fava, Sylvia. "Beyond Suburbia." *Annals of the American Association of Political and Social Science*, 42, November pp. 10-24.

Feinstein, O. "Why Ethnicity?" In Hartman, D., (ed.), *Immigrants and Migrants: The Detroit Ethnic Experience*. Detroit Center for Urban Studies, Wayne State University, 1974

Fellin, Phillip, and Eugene Litwak. "Neighborhood Cohesion Under Conditions of Mobility." *American Sociological Review* 28, June 1963, pp. 364-376.

Festinger, L., S. Schachter, and K. Back. *Social Pressures in Informal Groups*. New York: Harper and Bros., 1950.

Fischer, Claude S. "On Urban Alienation and Anomie: Powerlessness and Social Isolation." *American Sociological Review*, Vol. 38, June 1973, pp. 311-326.

_____ and Robert M. Jackson. "Suburbs, Networks, and Attitudes." In Barry Schwartz (ed.), *The Changing Face of the Suburbs*. Chicago: The University of Chicago Press, 1976.

Form, William H. and Nosow Sigmund. *Community in Disaster*. New York: Harper and Row, 1958.

Fox, J. R. "Therapeutic Rituals and Social Structure in Cohiti Pueblo." *Human Relations* 13 (4), November 1960, pp. 291-303.

Fried, Marc. "Grieving For a Lost Home." In L. J. Duhl (ed.), *The Urban Condition*. New York: Basic Books, 1963.

Fried, Marc, and Peggy Gleicher. "Some Sources of Residential Satisfaction in an Urban Slum." *Journal of the American Institute of Planners* 27, November 1961, pp. 305-315.

Friedson, Elliot. "Client Control and Medical Practice." *American Journal of Sociology* 65, January 1960, pp. 374-382.

_____. *Patient's Views of Mental Practice*. New York: Russell Sage, 1961.

_____. *Profession of Medicine*. New York: Dodd-Mead, 1970.

Gans, Herbert. "Urbanism and Suburbanism as Ways of Life: A Re-evaluation of Definitions." In *Human Behavior and Social Process*, pp. 625-648. Edited by Rose Arnold. Boston: Houghton Mifflin Company, 1962.

_____. *The Levittowners: Ways of Life and Politics in a New Suburban Community*. New York: Vintage Books, 1969.

_____. *The Urban Villagers: Group and Class in the Life of Italian Americans*. New York: The Free Press, 1962.

Gardner, Elmer, and Harontun Babigan. "The Longitudinal Comparison of Psychiatric Service." *American Journal of Orthopsychiatry* 36, October 1966, pp. 818-828.

Gartner, Alan, and Frank Rlessman. "Self-Help Models and Consumer Intensive Health Practice." *American Journal of Public Health*, 66, No.8, August 1976, pp. 783-786.

Glidewell, J. C. "A Social Psychology of Mental Health." In S. E. Golann & C. Eisdorfer (eds.), *Handbook of Community Mental Health*. New York: Appleton-Century-Crofts, 1972.

Goering, John and Rodney Coe. "Cultural Versus Situational Explanations of the Medical Behavior of the Poor." *Social Science Quarterly* 51 (2), September 1970, pp. 309-319.

Goffman. *Asylums*. New York: Anchor Press, 1961.

_____. *Stigma*. Englewood, California: Prentice Hall, 1963.

Golledge, R. G., and G. Zannaras. "Cognitive Approaches to the Analyis of Human Spatial Behavior." In W. H. Ittelson (ed.), *Environment and Cognition*. New York: Seminar Press, pp. 59-94.

Golledge, R. G., R. Briggs and D. Demko. "The Configuration of Distance in Intra-urban Space." *Proceedings of the Association of American Geographers*, pp. 60-66.

Gore, Susan. "The Influence of Social Support and Related Variables in Ameliorating the Consequences of Job Loss." Doctoral Dissertation, University of Pennsylvania, 1973.

Gottlieb, B. H. "The Contribution of Natural Support Systems to Primary Prevention Among Four Social Subgroups of Adolescent Males." *Adolescence* (1975), *X*, pp. 207-220.

_____. "Lay Influences on the Utilization and Provision of Health Services: A Review." *Canadian Psychological Review*, 17 (2) (1976): 126-136.

Gottlieb, Benjamin H., and Candice Schroter. "Resource Exchanges Between Professional and Natural Support Systems." *Professional Psychologist*. Volume 9. Number 4. November 1978, pp. 614-622.

Granovetter, Mark. "The Strength of Weak Ties." *American Journal of Sociology* 78, May 1973, pp. 1360-1380.

_____. "Granovetter Replies to Gans." *American Journal of Sociology*, 80, January 1975, pp. 527-529.

Graves, Forrest W. "Psychosomatic Symptoms Associated with Vital-Life Crises: An Exploratory Analysis of Self-Perceived Neighborhood

304

Contexts." Unpublished Master's Thesis, Eastern Michigan University, 1975.

Graves, Forrest W., "Social Support Versus Problem-Specific Helping: An Analysis of a Large-Scale Urban Sample." Doctoral Dissertation, Department of Sociology, Wayne State Universtiy, Detroit, Michigan, June, 1979.

Gurian, Bennett S., and Marjorie H. Cantor. "Mental Health and Community Support Systems for the Elderly." In Gene Usdin and Charles J. Hofling, *Aging: The Process and the People*. New York: Brunner/Mazel Incorporated, 1978.

Gurin, Gerald, Joseph Veroff, and Sheila Feld. *Americans View Their Mental Health*. Monograph No. 4. Joint Commission on Mental Illness and Health. New York: Basic Books, 1960.

Hall, A. L., and P.G. Bourne. "Indigenous Therapists in a Southern Black Community." *Archives of General Psychiatry* 28 (1973): 137-142.

Hall, James, K. Smith, and A. Bradley. "Delivering Mental Health Services to the Urban Poor." *Social Work*, 15, April 1970, pp. 108-115.

Hanley, Amos. *Human Ecology*. Boston: Beacon Press, 1950.

Hillery, George A., Jr. "Definitions of Community: Areas of Agreement." *Rural Sociology*, 20, June 1955, p. 118.

Hochschild, Arlie Russell. *The Unexpected Community*. Berkeley: University of California Press, 1973.

Hollingshead, August and Fredrick Redlich. *Social Class and Mental Illness: A Community Study*. New York: John Wiley and Sons, 1958.

Holmes, T. Stevenson and Thomas H. Holmes. "Short-Term Intrusions Into the Life Style Routine." *Journal of Psychosomatic Research*, XIV, September 1969, pp. 121-132.

Holmes, Thomas H., and Richard H. Rahe. "The Social Readjustment Rating Scale." *Journal of Psychosomatic Research*, XI, June 1967, pp. 212-218.

Homans, George C. *The Human Group*. New York: Harcourt, Brace, 1950.

Kahn, Robert L. "Supports of the Elderly: Family/Friends/Professionals." Research Proposal Draft, 1979.

Klein, Donald. *Community Dynamics and Mental Health*. New York: John Wiley and Sons, 1968.

_____. "Perceived Distance as a Function of Direction in the City." *Environment and Behavior*, 2 (1970): 40-51.

Leighton, Alexander. *My Name is Legion*. The Stirling County Studies. Vol. 1. New York: Basic Books, 1959.

Levy, Leo and Harold Visotsky. "The Quality of Urban Life: An analysis From the Perspective of Mental Health," In Henry Schmandt and Warner Bloomberg (eds.), *The Quality of Urban Life*. Urban Affairs Annual Reviews. Vol. 3. Beverly Hills, California: Sage Publications, 1969: pp. 255-268.

Levy, Leo H. "Self-Help Groups: Types and Psychological Processes." *The Journal of Applied Behavioral Science, 12*, (1976): 310-322.

Liebow, Elliot. *Tally's Corner*. Boston: Little, Brown and Company, 1967.

Lief, Alfred. *The Commonsense Psychiatry of Dr. Adolf Meyer*. New York: McGraw-Hill 1948, p. 433.

Liem, J. H. and R. Leim. "Life Events, Social Supports and Physical and Psychological Well-Being." Unpublished paper presented at the 84th annual meeting of the American Psychological Association, 1976.

Litwak, Eugene. "Occupational Mobility and Extended Family Cohesion." *American Sociological Review* 25, February 1960, pp. 9-21.

_____. "Geographical Mobility and Extended Family Cohesion." *American Sociological Review* 25, June 1960, pp. 385-394.

_____. "Voluntary Associations and Neighborhood Cohesion." *American Sociological Review* 26, April 1961, pp. 358-271.

_____ and Josephina Figuera. "Technological Innovation and Theoretical Functions of Primary Groups and Bureaucratic Structures." *American Journal of Sociology* 73, January 1968, pp. 468-481.

_____ and Henry Meyer. "A Balance Theory of Co-ordination Between Bureaucratic Organization and Community Primary Groups." Administrative Science Quarterly 2, June 1966, pp. 33-58.

_____ and Ivan Szelenyi. "Primary Group Structures and Their Functions: Kin, Neighbors, and Friends." *American Sociological Review* 34, August 1969 pp. 465-481.

_____, Earl Shiroi, Libby Zimmerman, and Jessie Bernstein. "Community Participation in Bureaucratic Organizations: Principles and Strategies." *Interchange* 1 (1970): 44-60.

_____, John E. Dono, *et al.* "An Empirical and Theoretical Statement of the Differential Functions and Structures of Primary Groups Amongst the Aged." Paper presented at the Annual Meeting of the American Sociological Association, Boston, Massachusetts, August 1979.

_____. *The Helping Networks of the Elderly.* New York Columist University Press, 1986.

Mayer, Mary J. "Kin and Neighbors: Differential Roles in Differing Cultures." Paper presented at the 29th Annual Gerontological Society Meeting, New York, New York, October 1976.

Parsons, Talcott. "An Outline of the Social System." In *Theories of Society, Foundations of Modern Sociological Theory*, pp. 30-79. Edited by Talcott Parsons, Edward Shils, Kasper Naegele, and Jesse Pitts. New York: The Free Press, 1961.

Pasley, S. "The Social Readjustment Rating Scale: A Study of the Significance of Life Events in Age Groups Ranging from College Freshman to Seventh Grade." Paper presented as part of a Tutorial in psychology, Chatham College, Pittsburgh, 1969.

Patterson, Shirley L. "Older Natural Helpers: These Characteristics and Patterns of Helping." *Public Welfare*, Fall 1971, pp. 400-403.

_____. "Toward a Conceptualization of Natural Helping." *Hreté*. University of South Carolina, Spring 1977, Vol. 4, No. 3, pp. 161-173.

Phillips, Derek. "The True Prevalence of Mental Illness in a New England State." *Community Mental Health Journal* 2/2, Spring 1966.

_____, and Bernard Segal. "Sexual Status and Psychiatric Symptoms." *American Sociological Review* 34 (1), February 1969, pp. 58-72.

_____. "Rejection: A Possible Consequence of Seeking Help for Mental Disorders." *American Sociological Review*, 28 (6), December 1963, pp. 963-972.

Pouissant, Alvin F. "Black Roadblocks to Black Unity." *Negro Digest*, 18 November 1968, pp. 11-19.

Powell, James J. "The Use of Self-Help Groups as Supportive Reference Communities." *American Journal of Orthopsychiatry* 45, (1975): 756-764.

President's Commission on Mental Health. Volume I. Washington, D.C.: U.S. Government Printing Office, 1978.

Rahe, Richard H. "Social Stress and Illness Onset." *Journal of Psychosomatic Research*, VIII, February 1964, pp. 35-44.

_____, and Thomas H. Holmes. "Social Psychological and Psychophysiological Aspects of Inguinal Hernia." *Journal of Psychosomatic Research*, VIII, July 1965, pp. 487-491.

_____. "Life-Change Measurement as a Predictor of Illness." *Proceedings of the Royal Society of Medicine*, LXI, May 1968, pp. 1124-1126.

Reiss, Albert. "Rural-Urban Status Differences in Inter-Personal Contacts." *American Journal of Sociology* 65, September 1959, pp. 182-195.

Richart, Robert and Lawrence Miller. "Factors Influencing Admission to a Community Mental Health Center." *Community Mental Health Journal* 4 (1), February 1969, pp. 27-35.

Roethlisberger, F. J. and W. J. Dickson. *Management and the Worker: Social Versus Technical Organization in Industry*. Cambridge: Harvard University Press, 1939.

Rosenberg, Morris. *The Logic of Survey Analysis*. New York: Basic Books, Inc., 1968.

Rosenblatt, Daniel and Edward Suchman. "The Underutilization of Medicalcare Services by Blue Collarites." In Arthur Shostak and William Gomberg (eds.,) *Blue Collar World: Studies of the American Worker*. Englewood-Cliffs, New Jersey: Prentice Hall, 1964, pp. 3341-349.

Rosengren, William and Mark Lefton (eds.). *Organization and Clients*. Columbus, Ohio: Charles E. Merrill Publishing Company, 1970.

_____. "The Careers of Clients and Organizations." In Rosengren and Lefton (eds.), *op cit*.

Rosow, Irving, *Social Integration of the Aged*. New York: Free Press, 1967.

_____. *Socialization to Old Age*. Berkeley: University of California Press, 1974.

Ruffini, Julio L., Harry F. Todd Jr., *et al.* "The Impact of an Outreach and I. & R. Program of the Elderly." Medical Anthropology Program, University of California, no date (assumed to be 1979).

_____ and Harry F. Todd Jr., "A Network Model for Leadership Development Among the Elderly." *The Gerontologist*. Volume 19. Number 2 (1979): 158-162.

Rutzen, Robert, "The Social Distribution of Primary Social Isolation Among the Aged: A Subcultural Approach." Paper presented at the Annual Meeting of the American Sociological Association, 1976.

308

Smith, Joel and Herman Turk. "Age and Some Behavioral and Attitudinal Aspects of Urban Community Integration." In Ida Harper Simpson (ed.), *Social Aspects of Aging*. Durham, N. C.: The Duke University Press, 1966, pp. 243-253.

Tannenbaum, Deborah. "People with Problems: Seeking Help in an Urban Community." Research Paper No. 64, Centre for Urban and Community Studies, University of Toronto, 1974.

Todd, D. M. "Contrasting Adaptations to the Social Environment of a High School: Implications of a Case Study of Helping Behavior in Two Adolescent Subcultures." In J. G. Kelly, *et al.* (eds.), *The High School: Students and Social Contexts in Two Midwestern Communities*. Community Psychology Series. No. 4. New York: Behavioral Publications, Inc., 1977.

Todd, David. "Helping Behavior for Citizens and Tribe: A Case Study of Two Adolescent Subcultures of a High School." Ph. D. Dissertation, University of Michigan, 1971.

Tolsdorff, Christopher. "Social Networks, Support and Coping: An Exploratory Study." *Family Process* 15 (4) 1976: 407-417.

Tomeh, Aida. "Informal Group Participation and Residential Patterns." *American Journal of Sociology* 70 (July 1964): 28-35.

Warren, Donald I. "Neighborhood Structure and Riot Behavior in Detroit: Some Exploratory Findings." Social Problems, 16, 4 (Spring 1969).

_____. "Neighborhoods in Urban Arenas," in *The Encyclopedia of Social Work*, New York: National Association of Social Work, 1971: 772-782.

_____. *Black Neighborhoods: An Assessment of Community Power*. An Arbor: The University of Michigan Press, 1975.

_____. *The Radical Center: The Politics of Alienation*, Notre Dame, Indiana: The University of Notre Dame Press, 1976.

_____. "Social Bonds in the Metropolitan Community," Paper Read at the Meeting of the Cross-Societal Comparative Research Project on the Residential Area Bond in Vienna Austria, April 4-6, 1977.

_____. "The Neighbor Factor in Problem Coping, Help Seeking and Social Support: Research Findings and Suggested Policy Implications," Paper presented at the 55th Annual Meeting of the American Orthopsychiatric Association San Francisco, California, March 1978.

_____. *Neighborhood and Community Contexts in Help Seeking, Problem Coping, and Mental Health: Data Analysis Monograph*. Ann Arbor: Program in Community Effectiveness, 1976.

_____ and Clifford, David. "Invoked Expertise and Neighborhood Type: Two Critical Dimensions in the Coordination of Bureaucratic Service Organizations and Primary Groups." Paper presented at the 69th Annual Meeting of the American Sociological Association, Montreal, Canada, August 1974.

_____ and Rachelle B. "The Helping Roles of Neighbors: Some Empirical Patterns." Paper presented at the 71st Annual Meeting of the American Sociological Association, Chicago, Illinois, September 1977.

_____ and Rachelle B. "Six Types of Neighborhoods," Psychology Today, Vol. 9, No. 1, June 1975: 74-79.

_____ and Rachelle B. "The Helping Roles of Neighbors: Some Empirical Patterns." Paper presented at the 71st Annual Meeting of the American Sociological Association, Chicago, Illinois, September 1977.

_____ and Rachelle B. "Six Types of Neighborhoods," Psychology Today, Vol. 9, No. 1, June 1975: 74-79.

Warren, Rachelle and Donald Warren. *The Neighborhood Organizer's Handbook*. Notre Dame: University of Notre Dame Press.

Weiss, Robert, and Bernard Berger. "Social Supports and the Reduction of Psychiatric Disability." *Psychiatry* 31 (2) (May 1968): 107-115.

_____, "The Fund of Sociability." *Transaction* 6 (July 1969): 36-43.

Welllman, Barry, *et al.* "The Uses of Community: Community Ties and Support Systems." Research Paper No. 47, Center for Urban and Community Studies, University of Toronto.

_____, P.,Craven and M. Whitaker. "Community Ties and Support Systems: From Intimacy to Support." In L. S. Bourne, (ed.), *The Form of Cities in Canada*. University of Toronto Department of Geography.

_____. "The Community Question." Research Paper No. 90, Center for Urban and Community Studies, University of Toronto.

_____ and Craven, Paul. "Informal Interpersonal Relations and Social Networks," *Sociological Inquiry*, 43, 3/4 1973.

_____. "Urban Connections." Research Paper #84, Centre for Urban and Community Studies, University of Toronto, 1976.

_____. "The Community Question: The Intimate Networks of East Yorkers," Centre for Urban and Community Studies, University of Toronto, April 1978.

310

_____, Paul Craven, Marilyn Whitaker, Sheila Dutoit, and Harvey Stevens. Community Ties and Support Systems. Center for Urban Research, paper #1 July 1971.

Whittle, William H., Jr. The Organization Man. New York: Simon & Schuster, 1956.

Wireman, Peggy. "Meanings of Community of Modern America." Unpublished Doctoral Dissertation: The American University, Department of Sociology, Washington, D. C., 1976.

Wirth, Louis. "Urbanism as a Way of Life." *American Journal of Sociology*, 44 (July 1938: 3-24.

Young, Michael and Willmot, Peter. *Family and Kinship in East London.* 2nd Edition. Harmondsworth, Middlesex, England: Penguin Books.

Zald, Mayer N. "Demographics, Politics, and the Future of the Welfare State." *Social Services Review* (March 1977).

Zola, Irving. Illness Behavior of the the Working Class." In Arthur Shostak and William Gombert (eds.), *Blue Collar World: Studies of the American Worker.* Englewood Cliffs: Prentice-Hall, 1964.

_____. "Culture and Symptoms--An Analysis of Patients Presenting Complaints." *American Sociological Review* 31 (5) (October 1966).

STUDIES IN HEALTH AND HUMAN SERVICES